AGAINST TIDE

A Generation Equipped to Turn the Tide of Our Culture

Preschool - 4th Grade
Second Edition

JULIE HIRAMINE
MEGAN BRIGGS

Cover Design:
David Rhody for Ti22, Inc.

Against the Tide Elementary: A Curriculum Guide to Raise Virtuous Children in Today's World

Copyright © 2005 by Generations of Virtue
Second Edition © 2010 by Generations of Virtue
Second Edition Revised 2013

Published by: Generations of Virtue
            P.O. Box 1353
            Monument, CO 80132

Printed in the United States of America

ISBN: 978-0-9766143-4-0

Table of Contents

You can order all of the resources
featured in this guide online at
www.generationsofvirtue.org

INTRO

When I was about 4, I tried to follow my brother and sister out into the ocean on a relatively calm afternoon. They were much older than I was and easily slipped past the crashing waves coming toward the shore. I inched out after them too soon, only to find a wave towering over my small frame. To my small stature the wave looked ten feet tall! Looking up at the wall of water that would come crashing down on me at any moment, I felt tiny in comparison. I had no idea what to do in this situation. I was not prepared for this moment.

As I grew older, I was taught by my family how to navigate the surf. I learned how to dive under the waves that pummeled the shore and swim through the crashing breakers. I became skilled at swimming in the ocean no matter what the day might bring. I learned when I was very young to dive under the waves on days that the tide was easy and the waves were small and gentle. As I grew older, I felt comfortable even when the waves towered over me at six and eight feet. I learned the nuances of skirting a rip tide and body surfing through the churning surf. I acquired the skill of knowing where the wave was going to break and whether to go under or over it. I built up my confidence so that I felt at ease in the powerful ocean. I could read the tide like a map and react accordingly.

What I experienced when I was only 4 is the exact dilemma that our children face in our culture today. They are tiny in comparison to the waves of life that are coming their way to crash down upon them. While others seem to slip into the tide of our culture unharmed, they feel dwarfed by the immeasurable disparity between God's word and the attitude of our day. We as parents need to be the ones to train them and prepare them to swim against the tide. We need to equip and empower them to face the tidal wave that is building up, wanting to sweep them away with its destructive power.

Our job is to prepare them for the moment when they will be faced with powerful opposition to what they have been taught. There will come a day that is sooner than we can comprehend when the onslaught of cultural baggage will cascade upon them. They will be young and impressionable when this occurs. Only the ones who have been prepared by the Lord and their parents will be able to stand. This next generation has a mandate not only to stand firm, but to stand firm against the tide that is swelling in around them, threatening to sweep them off their feet into the cultural norm. It is our job as parents to train them up to face this deluge, teaching them how to dive under and swim beyond the insistent waves of promiscuity, pornography, indecency, and unhealthy relationships. They need to know how to navigate the turbulent surf of the adolescent years and swim to the calm waters of God's divine plan for healthy relationships and, ultimately, marriage or God's call on their life.

God has given us a mandate as parents to raise a generation that will be pure in heart and follow the precepts of His Word with a passion. I see a generation that will run into the waves of this culture without fear because they know their God and are willing to hold high His banner and His standard. They are equipped and prepared to not only swim against the tide, but to turn the tide back to God's standard and His design. We do not want to raise our children to cower in a corner with their standards, but rather, we want them to be the leaders in the hand of the Almighty God to change our world. Therefore, they have a big job ahead of them and that job begins with us as parents, when they are young. It is time now to start setting the paradigm so they will be prepared for the moment the first wave threatens to crash upon them. God is in the business of raising up a Generation of Virtue.

Dear Parents

You are about to embark on a very special journey with your child. Against the Tide is an incredible resource to help you build a firm relationship with your child. This paves the way for communication about important issues your child will face and how to establish healthy relationships for a lifetime. You are the expert God has appointed to teach your child virtuous living, sex education, and purity. This can start in preschool as your child begins to learn about his or her body and continue into elementary school as your child matures.

This curriculum guide is for preschool through fourth grade. We divided it up this way because in fifth grade, this program becomes more intensive as your child goes through puberty. (There is a separate curriculum guide for grades 5 – 8.)

During these early formative years, it is important that you use this curriculum as a guideline only. You know your child and you know his or her maturity level. You are the ultimate expert on what to share with your child and when to talk about each issue. We encourage you to do it sooner rather than later. It always feels early to us as parents, but we want to be the first ones to share the message because the first message is the most powerful. We cannot consider our children sheltered just because we regulate their influences while in our care. They still have friends in their neighborhoods and see many different children at church. It is safe to assume that they are receiving messages from many different sources. The most important message they will receive is from you, their parents. This is your opportunity to make a difference and stand in opposition to our culture's immoral standards.

One small detail is that, for practical reasons, we have often referred to your child as "he" throughout this curriculum guide. No offense to your daughters is intended by this!

May God richly bless you as you prepare your family to raise a standard of purity in this generation.

Julie Hiramine

DeaR PastoR

You are about to embark on a very special journey with the children you teach and their parents. Against the Tide is an incredible resource to help you build a firm foundation of purity in your students' lives. The curriculum is perfect for MOPs groups, homeschool groups, Bible studies, Sunday school, the church library, cell groups, church preschools and schools, and as a tool to train and equip your students' parents and your volunteers who work closely with these children.

As you work through the resources featured in the guide, you will be paving the way for communication about important issues your students will face and how to establish healthy relationships for a lifetime. Purity training starts in preschool as your students are learning things like creation and basic manners, and the training continues throughout the elementary years.

This curriculum guide is for preschool through fourth grade. There is a second curriculum guide for 5-8th grade. It is divided this way because in fifth grade the program becomes more intensive as your students go through puberty and begin facing more and more pressure from our culture.

During these early formative years, it is important to use this curriculum as a guideline only. You know your students and you know their maturity level regarding issues of purity and sex education. As we have written this guide it is our heart that the parents be the key source of information especially when it comes to talking about sex. Encourage parents to establish this connection with their precious children and take advantage of the privilege it is to share with them about one of God's special gifts to husbands and wives in a marriage relationship.

Be sensitive to God's leading as you decide when to share with your students and what to talk about concerning each issue. We encourage you to do it sooner rather than later. It always feels early to us as teachers, but we know that the first message a child receives is always the most impacting, and we cannot consider our children sheltered just because they go to church. They still have friends in their neighborhoods and interact with many different children at school, in the community, and while at church. It is safe to assume that they are receiving messages from many different sources.

One small detail is that, for practical reasons, we have often referred to your students as "he" throughout this curriculum guide. No offense to the girls is intended by this!

May God richly bless you as you prepare your students to raise a standard of purity in this generation.

Julie Hiramine

THE ORGANIZER

Against the Tide Elementary takes you year by year through resources you can use to teach your children to stand against the tide of culture. We strive to make the curriculum as easy for mom or dad to implement as possible. At the beginning of each grade, you'll find an Organizer that will lead you through the resources featured that year. The Organizer is kind of like a beach bag; it's the first thing you pack and the first thing you reach for when you go to the beach. The Organizer keeps all your notes for the year in one easy reference place. Listed below, we'll walk you through the layout of an Organizer and how you can use it to your full advantage.

Tools for the Sandbox

☐ This list shows you all the resources—children's and parent's—you will need for this year.

☐

☐

☐

☐

Message in a Bottle

A handy space for you to write notes for future reference. You might jot down which resources you already own, which ones you'll need to purchase, and what you really want to focus on that year.

Lifeguard Watch - *Things your children should learn this year*

- These are the basic principles your children will be learning this year after going through the resources we recommend. This list is kind of like a progress report for your kids. Did they understand the lesson about saving their first kiss for their wedding day from *The Princess and the Kiss*? If not, you might consider going back to that book.

Just Joining Us?

If this is your first year implementing the *Against the Tide* curriculum, we've included a list of resources we recommend starting with, before you launch into the resources featured in that grade. As preschool is the first grade, we did not include a "Just Joining Us?" section in that grade.

TIMELINE OPTIONS

These are different schedules we've worked out for you to go through the children's resources featured in each grade. We purposefully left out scheduling the reading for mom and dad (we didn't think you would appreciate homework assignments!). Mom and dad are free to go through their books at their own pace.

Option 1 – Week Study

If you wanted to do all the resources in one week, this timeline divides the books across 5 days. Most of the books we feature in *Against the Tide Elementary* are short; however, some of them will take you longer than one week to finish. For these particular resources, we give you a heads up to let you know that they will take longer than the week allotted in option 1. Because this track only takes you a week, you might want to implement it once in the fall and then in the spring you can revisit your favorite books or even add your favorites to your family library.

Option 2 – Unit Study

We've organized the unit study to divide the resources across four weeks. There are a handful of resources we've featured that will most likely take you longer than four weeks to get through. We have made notes for you on these particular resources; giving you a heads up that you will need to keep working on those after the unit study is complete.

Option 3 – Family Devos

This option is for families who are interested in incorporating the resources into their regular family devotion time. For this option, we list the resources you can enjoy together as a family, and then point out the ones you probably want to do one-on-one with your children. While every family has different dynamics, we've found that the resources that specifically address issues of sexuality and body development are best covered one-on-one with your children. However, use your discretion with these books. Perhaps you have a family of all boys, relatively close in age. It might be totally appropriate to cover books like *The Wonderful Way Babies Are Made* as a family. We leave that up to your discretion.

Preschool

Intro

Your child's preschool years consist of precious moments you can use to create a firm foundation for physical, emotional, and spiritual purity. During this age, your child is extremely impressionable, and the more positive values you can instill in your child the better. Don't miss the opportunities that come up to talk to your children about the lessons you will be teaching them through the books featured this year. The information may seem like it's going over their heads, but it's really not.

Memory Verse
"Keep yourself pure."
1 Timothy 5:22 (NKJV)

GODLY SEXUALITY

This year focuses on foundational truths about sexuality. Truths such as: God created you. He created your body and your spirit. Everything God makes is good and its purpose is to glorify Him. Take advantage of your child's openness at this stage of development and keep an open conversation about the fact that God made him or her.

MEDIA DISCERNMENT

When your children are really young, be sensitive about media that contains humor that only adults understand. Sometimes this humor is innocent—an allusion to politics or cultural references—but other times there is humor that is intended to be inappropriate. Whether your child understands the full meaning of this humor or not, this kind of humor is harmful. What these subtle, inappropriate messages do is familiarize children with inappropriate content. But the truth is, no matter how old they are or what they understand, they should never really be comfortable with it. Look for movies, audio books, stories, and songs that tell valuable tales and teach good lessons.

SPIRITUAL DEVELOPMENT

One of the greatest lessons a child can learn is to respect God-given authority. When children learn to respect and obey their parents, they are learning, in essence, to respect and obey God—the ultimate authority. God has designed the parent-child relationship as a training ground to teach the all-important principle of respecting authority. While this does not give you an excuse for a parental power-trip, it's important to teach your children to obey you because it's not so much about them obeying you as it is them learning to obey God.

TEACHABLE MOMENTS

Take advantage of situations that come up in the media your children are exposed to. For instance, some movies—even if they are age appropriate—portray unhealthy relationships or actions. For example, some Disney movies contain kissing when the couple is not married. This is a good time to illuminate this point and thereby teach your children moral values of purity. I make an effort to point this out to them by saying, "Hey, are they married yet?" when there is a scene with kissing or holding hands, etc. By bringing this to their attention at a young age, they won't think that everything they see in movies or on TV is acceptable for them to do as well.

Preschool Organizer

Tools for the Sandbox

- [ ] *A Little Boy after God's Own Heart*
  by Jim and Elizabeth George
- [ ] *A Little Girl after God's Own Heart*
  by Elizabeth George
- [ ] *Good Manners for a Little Princess*
  by Kelly Chapman
- [ ] *Good Manners for a Little Warrior*
  by Kelly Chapman
- [ ] *My Big Book of 5-Minute Devotions*
  by Pamela Kennedy with
  Douglas Kennedy
- [ ] *The Swimsuit Lesson*
  by Jon Holsten
- [ ] *The Wonderful Way Babies Are Made*
  by Larry Christenson
- [ ] *Guardians of Purity*
  by Julie Hiramine
- [ ] *Project Blessing*
  by Kay and Julie Hiramine

Message in a Bottle

_____

_____

_____

_____

_____

_____

_____

_____

_____

_____

Lifeguard Watch - *Things your children should learn this year*

- [ ] How God made the world
- [ ] Basic concept of how living things reproduce
- [ ] Issues of creation and reproduction are totally appropriate to talk about with mom or dad
- [ ] Where it is appropriate to be touched
- [ ] Where it is not appropriate to be touched
- [ ] What to do if someone touches them inappropriately
- [ ] Basic table manners
- [ ] Basic hygiene principles: brushing their teeth, combing their hair, washing their faces
- [ ] How to pick up their toys
- [ ] How to make a friend feel welcome and included in play dates
- [ ] How to share their toys
- [ ] Basic concept of the fruit of the Spirit

TIMELINE OPTIONS

Option 1 – Week Study

Start each day by having your child repeat the memory verse back to you. Your goal is to have them saying the verse from memory by the end of the week.

Day 1: *Good Manners for a Little Princess* and/or *Good Manners for a Little Warrior* and one devotion from *My Big Book of 5-Minute Devotions**

Day 2: *The Wonderful Way Babies Are Made* (first half) and one devotion from *My Big Book of 5-Minute Devotions*

Day 3: *The Wonderful Way Babies Are Made* (second half) and one devotion from *My Big Book of 5-Minute Devotions*

Day 4: *A Little Boy after God's Own Heart* and/or *A Little Girl after God's Own Heart* and one devotion from *My Big Book of 5-Minute Devotions*

Day 5: *The Swimsuit Lesson* and one devotion from *My Big Book of 5-Minute Devotions*

**My Big Book of 5-Minute Devotions* is going to take you longer than one week to complete. The week-long study will take you through five devotions, and then you will have 36 more devotions to finish after you complete the week study.

Option 2 – Unit Study

Start each session by having your child repeat the memory verse back to you. Your goal is to have them saying the verse from memory by the end of the unit.

Week 1: *Good Manners for a Little Princess* and/or *Good Manners for a Little Warrior* and 5 devotions from *My Big Book of 5-Minute Devotions**

Week 2: *The Wonderful Way Babies Are Made* and 5 devotions from *My Big Book of 5-Minute Devotions*

Week 3: *A Little Boy after God's Own Heart* and/or *A Little Girl after God's Own Heart* and 5 devotions from *My Big Book of 5-Minute Devotions*

Week 4: *The Swimsuit Lesson* and 5 devotions from *My Big Book of 5-Minute Devotions*

**My Big Book of 5-Minute Devotions* is going to take you longer than four weeks to complete. The unit study will take you through the first 20 devotions, and then you will have 21 remaining.

Option 3 – Family Devos

All of the books for children featured in this grade are appropriate to incorporate into family devotions, with the exception of *The Wonderful Way Babies Are Made*. While teaching children about how God made us and how He makes babies is not a shameful subject, please use discretion with this resource. Some children are not comfortable talking about these issues with siblings, especially if the siblings are older. However, we have known families who have children close in age and the same gender who have enjoyed this particular book together. Please use your best judgment.

The Wonderful Way Babies are Made

by Larry Christenson

This is a wonderful book for kids 3-10. The big text is for younger kids, while the text in the boxes should be saved for older, more mature kids. Each set of text communicates the wonder of God's creation as it tells the story of how God created the world, how He made plants, animals, people, and families, and the wonderful way He makes babies. We love this book because it gives children a Godly, positive perspective on creation and life. It also has a profound section on adoption and explains how Jesus was adopted by Joseph and Mary.

Make sure you read the **BIG** text in this book. The other text—in the boxes—is for older, more mature children and should be saved for a later grade. Also, be careful about letting your child look at this book alone if he or she can read.

Activities & Discussion Questions

Don't you think it's wonderful that God has the power to make anything He wants?

Do you know that God made you special and unique?

How many different kinds of plants and animals do you think there are in the world?

Let's thank God right now for all the wonderful things He made. You can especially thank Him for your favorite things.

Draw pictures of 5 things God created.

If you have pictures from the day your child was born, show them to your child and tell him the story of the day he was born. Remember to tell him that he is very special and he is unique from anyone else. You might want to mention things like "God blessed us very much when He gave you to us."

THE SWIMSUIT LESSON

by Jon Holsten

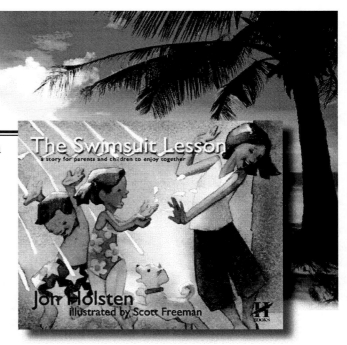

This is a unique storybook that has a very important message to share. Jon Holsten is a veteran police officer who has investigated and prosecuted child molesters. He is passionate about helping parents educate their children about sexual abuse, thereby reducing their children's risk of being victimized. The story follows a mother and her two children as she relates to them the "swimsuit lesson," which states that it is inappropriate for anyone to touch you in the places your swimsuit covers. The children also learn what to do if they are ever inappropriately touched. This book includes a Parent's Guide which is full of great advice to help parents effectively communicate the vital information in the story. This is an excellent resource to implement as you begin the conversation about sexual abuse. I observed my children were engaged in the story and able to understand the principles, while not being threatened or alarmed by the topic.

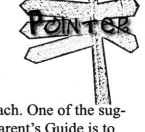

Read the Parent's Guide in the back of the book before you read the story to your children, as it will help you prepare for the lesson you are about to teach. One of the suggestions included in the Parent's Guide is to have your children wear their swimsuits while reading this book so that they can know exactly where it is inappropriate to be touched.

DISCUSSION QUESTIONS

What did Mark and Lisa learn in this story?

Tell me in your own words what the "swimsuit lesson" is.

What should you do if someone touches you where your swimsuit covers?

When is it appropriate (explain what this word means) for someone to touch you where your swimsuit covers? And who is allowed to touch you here?

MY BIG BOOK OF 5-MINUTE DEVOTIONS

by Pamela Kennedy with Douglas Kennedy

Full of short devotions for little ones, this book will enthrall your child with all its pictures and fun facts about animals. Each devotion time includes scripture and discussion points to teach children how to study the Word and pray. Every devotion highlights a different animal and points out something in their nature that corresponds to the One who created them.

These devotions literally take 5 minutes to read and discuss. The authors have done an excellent job providing valuable instruction through Biblical principles while keeping their points short and accessible for little children. Be sure to engage your child in conversation using the discussion questions provided.

ACTIVITIES

If there is a particular animal your child takes interest in, help him or her research the animal. Take the opportunity to engage your child in learning about something that captures his or her attention. You could even incorporate a trip to the zoo!

Have your son or daughter draw a picture of one of the animals from the book and something that represents what that particular devotion taught him or her about God's Word.

BOOKS NOT TO MISS for Girls

GOOD MANNERS FOR A LITTLE PRINCESS

by Kelly Chapman

Kendall and Caroline are sisters who learn about the manners that princesses practice. Told in a cute way, they learn about table manners, using "please" and "thank you", sharing, and above all, treating others with respect and kindness. This book does an excellent job explaining to young ladies that manners are really about the Golden Rule and respecting other people. Your daughter will love the princess theme and the entertaining drawings in this book.

POINTER: This book includes a "Pretty Please Princess Tea Pop Quiz" in the back. It's a fun way to engage your daughters in learning good manners!

How do you think Caroline did responding to her sister's cranky mood? Is there something she could have done differently?

What makes someone a princess?

What are the Golden Rules Kendall and Caroline learn about?

DISCUSSION QUESTIONS

A LITTLE GIRL AFTER GOD'S OWN HEART

by Elizabeth George

Take your daughter through the fruit of the Spirit in rhyming prose. Everyday presents new opportunities for little girls to choose patience over hastiness, love over hatred, and self-control over temper-tantrums. This beautiful book makes a lesson in Godly character fun and rewarding. This charming book is perfect for reading during the day or at bedtime.

POINTER: Point out instances where your daughter can demonstrate a fruit of the Spirit after reading this book. If you notice her demonstrating one, be sure to let her know. If there was an opportunity where she could have made a better choice, explain how she could have practiced a fruit of the Spirit in that situation.

Read Galatians 5:22 and 23 with your daughter.

After reading about the fruit of the Spirit in the Bible, ask your daughter to say in her own words what each of the fruits mean.

DISCUSSION QUESTIONS

Books Not To Miss for Boys

Good Manners for a Little Warrior

by Kelly Chapman

Your son will enjoy joining Luke as he travels to the Warrior Prince Academy and learns how to be a code-keeper. Through a clever story line, boys will learn about the Golden rule, and the code that helps them interact politely with others. Covering the basics of table manners, watching your speech, being a good sport, using phrases like "excuse me" and "thank you", and how to treat others like you want to be treated, this book is fun and includes colorful pictures.

Pointer: This book makes it easy to point out what is good behavior and what is not. You can point out when your son is behaving well by saying things like "Good manners!" or "You are being a code-keeper!".

Discussion Questions

What makes someone a warrior?	*What do manners have to do with the Golden Rule?*	*How did you do on the quiz in the back of the book?*

A Little Boy After God's Own Heart

by Jim and Elizabeth George

This is a beautiful book full of character-building fun straight from scripture. Going through the fruit of the Spirit, your son will learn valuable lessons like: how to control his temper, be a good friend, take responsibility for the jobs he's been given, and much more. These wonderfully penned lessons in rhyming prose are suitable for school time and bedtime reading.

Pointer: Point out instances where your son can demonstrate a fruit of the Spirit after reading this book. If you notice him demonstrating one, be sure to let him know. If there was an opportunity where he could have made a better choice, explain how he could have practiced a fruit of the Spirit in that situation.

Discussion Questions/Activities

Read Galatians 5:22 and 23 with your son.	*After reading about the fruit of the Spirit in the Bible, ask your son to say in his own words what each of the fruits mean.*

GuaRDiaNs oF PuRiTY

by Julie Hiramine

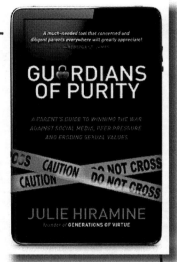

From her years of ministry experience - both with youth and parents - Julie has gleaned practical wisdom on what works and what doesn't when it comes to purity. One thing predominantly sticks out in Julie's book: Parents - you have incredible impact in the lives of your children! Covering the subjects of Godly sexuality, monitoring media influences, establishing convictions about romance and relationships, and intentionally blessing your children, Julie equips parents to be a positive influence on their children - specifically in the area of purity. This generation has a lot stacked up against them, but God is also determined to bring about His standard on the earth. It is the generation who has their parents and leaders on board with God's standard that is going to win this spiritual battle. Teach your children how to live out God's principles for purity, integrity, and destiny in Him as you partner with them in becoming a part of God's holy generation.

- *Guardians of Purity* was written for parents of children all ages. In its pages you'll find tips for toddlers, tweens, and teens. This is a book you will want to go back and reference time and again as your children mature.

- It's really important to discuss with your spouse what kind of standards you are going to embrace as a family. Take time to discuss things like: how you are going to talk about sex with your kids, what kind of media standards you will have (for your kids and yourselves), and how you can pray for each one of your kids. Remember to pray for them as a couple - there is power in coming together and lifting your kids up to the Lord. If your spouse is not avaialable, write your decisions down. Discuss them with a friend or mentor who is on the same page as you. Ask your friend to help you pray for your kids.

PROJECT BLESSING

by Kay and Julie Hiramine

Pulling research from various sources and drawing on personal experience in ministry and as parents, Kay and Julie Hiramine have compiled a simple how-to guide to make blessing a regular part of your family life. Whether your kids are quite young or about to leave your house, blessing is a practice that will help them succeed in whatever they are called to in God's Kingdom. Our culture is suffering from a lack of blessing, causing our children to seek other sources for acceptance, identity, and purpose. Parents are instrumental in pointing children to God as the ultimate giver of all these things. Kay and Julie invite you to stand in the gap for your kids as you ask for God's favor on their lives and as you speak into them words of acceptance they need for their spiritual, emotional, and physical well being.

POINTERS:

- Be sure to watch the DVD included with *Project Blessing*. It will help you start the blessing off if you are unsure what to do. This resource is also excellent for churches to use with their congregations.

- Sometimes parents feel unqualified to bless because they were not intentionally blessed as children. *Project Blessing* will help you work through common hindrances that keep people from blessing. Whether you are a single parent or married, God will qualify you and help you to see that blessing your children is one of the best things you can do for them.

Notes

Kindergarten Intro

A discussion on Godly sexuality should be an ongoing discussion you are having with your children. Don't make it something you save for a specific time in the school day and no other time. Your children need to know from your actions that the subject of sexuality is a completely safe subject to discuss with mom and dad. While it may not seem that important to discuss issues of sexuality with your kindergartner, this is the time you can lay a foundation for openness and honesty for later years. These years are incredibly important in your child's development as a person. The information and the example they learn from you now, while they are young, are going to shape their behavior and the choices they make as adolescents and teenagers, and eventually as adults.

Memory Verse
"I will praise You, for I am fearfully and wonderfully made." Psalm 139:14 (NKJV)

Points FOR KINDERGARTEN

GODLY SEXUALITY

Although we might not think about modesty being an issue for our young children, this is a good age to set a healthy standard for modesty. It is important to contemplate the implications of clothing choices when kids are young and how it will impact them when they are older. Many times we think our little girls look cute in a bikini, short skirts, or short shirts; however, it is crucial to look ahead and see how we feel about the same outfits as puberty arrives and our girls begin to develop into young ladies. If we do not feel comfortable with our teens wearing these clothes, we should not allow them to do it as children, either. As teenagers, your children might feel it is too much to suddenly change their dressing habits simply because they are getting older. Girls especially might feel ashamed of their bodies or feel something is wrong with the way they are developing if they suddenly have to cover up more. Concerning modesty, consistency throughout their development is key.

Another focus at this age is teaching your children about privacy. As they continue to mature, they need to know how to bathe alone and to shut the door when using the restroom. It's important for children to realize that there is a need for modesty and discretion concerning their bodies. If your children enjoy bathing together, one idea is to have them wear their swimsuits while playing in the tub.

MEDIA DISCERNMENT

If you are like me and my husband, you watch the news. We have noticed a need in our household, especially with our younger children, to be careful about leaving the news on all the time, "unsupervised". Little ones walking through the living room do not need to see some of the graphic images they show. Also, be especially careful when commercials come on. At our house, we either turn the tv off during the commercials or at least mute them.

SPIRITUAL DEVELOPMENT

Several of the resources we've included for Kindergarten address character development. Don't miss opportunities to strengthen your child's character by not only talking about it with him or her, but also providing a good example yourself. For instance, if you are trying to teach respect for authority, do you provide a good example of respecting the authority in your life? More than your words on the subject, your children will pick up on your actions and the example you give.

TEACHABLE MOMENTS

The books included in the Kindergarten curriculum, *Why Do Plants Grow?* and *The Story of Me,* will help you to make a discussion about Godly sexuality something that is not considered "taboo". This year, focus on using the proper name for body parts and pointing out the beauty of God's creation. Children benefit when they realize God has designed everything to reproduce in a similar way. It was His intention for all living things to reflect His glory and honor Him with their cycles and seasons of life.

KINDERGARTEN ORGANIZER

Tools for the Sandbox

- [ ] *I'd Be Your Hero*
        by Kathryn O'Brien
- [ ] *I'd Be Your Princess*
        by Kathryn O'Brien
- [ ] *The Princess & the Kiss*
        by Jennie Bishop
- [ ] *The Squire & the Scroll*
        by Jennie Bishop
- [ ] *The Story of Me*
        by Stan and Brenna Jones
- [ ] *Why Do Plants Grow?*
        by Susan Horner
- [ ] *Preparing Him for the Other Woman*
        by Sheri Rose Shepherd
- [ ] *Project Blessing* (see page 11)
        by Kay and Julie Hiramine
- [ ] *Shepherding a Child's Heart*
        by Tedd Tripp

Message in a Bottle

_____
_____
_____
_____
_____
_____
_____
_____
_____
_____

Lifeguard Watch - *Things your children should learn this year*

- [ ] My first kiss is a gift I should protect
- [ ] What makes someone a princess is her character
- [ ] What makes someone a prince is his character
- [ ] I am a unique creation and my parents treasure me
- [ ] God created me a boy or a girl
- [ ] The difference between boys and girls

- [ ] Basic concept of how plants reproduce
- [ ] God's Word is like a sword that you can use to fight temptation and make good
- [ ] choices
      God created all living things to reproduce
- [ ] in a similar way
      God's design for families
- [ ] Jesus taught some very important principles to live by

Just Joining Us?

If this is your first year doing the *Against the Tide* curriculum, there are a few resources we recommend starting with, before you jump into this year's resources:

- *The Wonderful Way Babies Are Made* (description on page 5)
- *The Swimsuit Lesson* (description on page 6)
- *Guardians of Purity* (description on page 10)

TIMELINE OPTIONS

Option 1 – Week Study

Start each day by having your child repeat the memory verse back to you. Your goal is to have them saying the verse from memory by the end of the week.

Day 1: *I'd Be Your Hero* and/or *I'd Be Your Princess*
Day 2: *The Story of Me*
Day 3: *The Princess and the Kiss*
Day 4: *Why Do Plants Grow?*
Day 5: *The Squire and the Scroll*

Option 2 – Unit Study

Start each session by having your child recite the memory verse with you. Your goal is to have them saying the verse from memory by the end of the unit.

Week 1: *I'd Be Your Hero* and/or *I'd Be Your Princess* and *The Story of Me*
Week 2: *The Princess and the Kiss*
Week 3: *Why Do Plants Grow?*
Week 4: *The Squire and the Scroll*

Option 3 – Family Devos

All of the children's books featured in this grade are appropriate to incorporate into your regular family devotions, with the exception of *The Story of Me*. This book is best done one-one-one. Be sure to recite your memory verse at the beginning or end of your family devotion time.

Royal Character

I'd Be Your Hero

by Kathryn O'Brien

This is a charming story for mothers and sons. The story follows an imaginative boy and his mother as they discuss key Godly characteristics every boy should emulate. Based on scripture, the story focuses on virtues such as strength, humility, love, and courage. Your son will love the daring pictures and catchy plot. More importantly, this book will help your son focus on the true heart of a prince.

POINTER: This book has excellent material for quality mother-son time. There are character points in this story you can point out when they come up in your son's life. Look for opportunities to encourage him as he strives to exemplify the characteristics of the young prince in the story.

Have you done something that makes you feel like a prince?	What are some things a prince does for other people?	**DISCUSSION QUESTIONS**
What makes someone a prince?	How can you act like a prince?	

I'd Be Your Princess

by Kathryn O'Brien

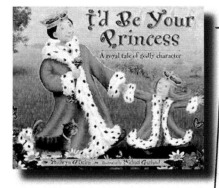

This charming story follows an imaginative girl seeking her father's approval for her actions and her character in general. The story includes 15 succinct lessons taken directly from scripture associated with the way a Godly little girl acts. Your daughter will love the catchy plot and magnificent drawings as she enjoys some quality father-daughter time. Another reason we like this book so much is because most girls really like the princess theme and our culture is currently pushing the wrong type of princess paradigm. This book will appeal to your daughter's interest in princesses while communicating to her the characteristics of a Godly princess.

POINTER:

This book makes for excellent father-daughter material. We like it because it's something dad can use to launch into a conversation about Godly character. Plus, there are specific character traits that come up in the story that you can point out when your daughter practices them.

Have you done something that makes you feel like a princess?	What are some things a princess does for other people?	**DISCUSSION QUESTIONS**
What makes someone a princess?	How can you act like a princess?	

THE STORY OF Me

by Stan and Brenna Jones

This is the first book in the *God's Design for Sex Series*, which is designed to take parents and children through age-appropriate sex education. Included in this book are discussions about the difference between boys and girls, anatomy, pregnancy, adoption, and more. The books are meant to be used as discussion openers for you and your children.

This book is meant for parent and child to go through together. Because of its format of a young boy talking to his parents about how God made him and how God designed his family, it makes for a very natural discussion opener for you and your children. The authors have done an excellent job making a conversation about Godly sexuality something that is not awkward or over your child's head.

ACTIVITIES & DISCUSSION QUESTIONS

> *How did God make you special?*

> *Do you think it's wonderful the way God made your body?*

> *Does He make other people special?*

> *What do you think your family will be like when you get married?*

Tell your child the story of the day he was born. If you have pictures from his day of birth, show him the pictures and narrate the story as creatively as you can. Start the story with something interesting, like, "It was a stormy day, but we made it to the hospital regardless of the weather." This way, your child will think that the story of his birth could also be worthy of being told in a storybook. Afterward, you could help him record his story in his own book and have him draw pictures for it.

The Princess & the Kiss

for boys and girls!

by Jennie Bishop

This is a charming tale about a young princess who saves her first kiss for her wedding day. This is a great story for both boys and girls, as the young suitor who eventually marries the princess has also saved his first kiss for his future wife. Specifically with girls, with all the princess paraphernalia currently circulating in our culture, this story does a wonderful job of relating to your daughter that she is a daughter of the King and that her worth comes from the Lord. *The Princess and the Kiss* is also available with audio CD.

POINTER

This would be an opportune time to explain to your child the importance of saving his first kiss for the one he marries. You should also explain to him that it is appropriate to kiss members of the family but not the kids at Sunday school, in the neighborhood, etc.

Activities & Discussion Questions

Did you enjoy this book?

What was your favorite part?

Which one was your favorite picture?

Are there any parts of the story you don't understand?

When I read this story to my daughter, she asked me where her first kiss was. Thinking quickly, I replied "I keep it in my heart". But as a way for your child to visualize the concept of saving his first kiss, you can have him decorate a box to keep his kiss in for safe keeping.

WHY DO PLANTS GROW?

by Susan Horner

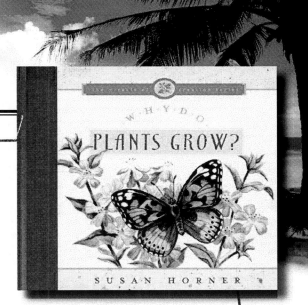

This is the first book in the *Miracle of Creation Series*. Susan Horner designed this series to gradually teach children about reproduction by starting with plants, moving to animals, and finally learning about human reproduction. She believes your child will understand these lessons better if he sees the way God created other organisms to reproduce as well. This book does an excellent job illuminating the fact that God created all living things to reproduce in a similar way. He was very purposeful about the way He designed us to function for His own glory. Susan makes a conversation about reproduction a natural and wonderful topic. Located in the back of this book are several activities for families to teach children about plants and reproduction.

POINTER

The author, Susan Horner, suggests reading the story in segments and interspersing the activities found in the back of the book with the reading. Also, since there is a relatively large amount of information for your child to absorb, we suggest reading this book a few times throughout the year.

DISCUSSION QUESTIONS

From the Family Fun Activities located in the back of the book:
Take a stick of celery with leaves and place it in a jar of water. Add a few drops of food coloring. After an hour, observe the celery. See how the celery stalk draws up the water to its leaves. You can also do this activity by using a natural white carnation. Find more activities on page 28.

What ways do plants reproduce in the same way that people do? Why do you think God decided to make plants reproduce this way?

What season are we in right now?

What stage are the plants in right now?

THE SQUIRE & THE SCROLL

for boys and girls!

by Jennie Bishop

This allegorical tale is for boys and girls of all ages. Much like *The Princess and the Kiss*, your child can capture the Biblical lessons found in this book, no matter what his age, as he follows the young squire on his quest to retrieve the Lantern of Purest Light. While on his journey, the young squire obeys the words of his precious Scroll, and this obedience allows him to resist the snares of the dragon and victoriously retrieve the Lantern. Your child will enjoy the medieval theme and captivating paintings as you share this book with him. *The Squire and the Scroll* is also available with audio CD.

POINTER

This book brings up an excellent opportunity to explain how God can use young people to change their society. The squire was able to retrieve the Lantern of Purest Light and defeat the dragon when no one else could. Don't forget to mention the fact that the squire was just a young helper, yet he was able to do what others could not because of his obedience to God's Word.

ACTIVITIES & DISCUSSION QUESTIONS

> Who was your favorite person in the story? Why do you like him or her?

> What was the story about?

> Did you know the Bible is called the "Sword of the Spirit"? Why do you think it's called that?

Read Hebrews 4:12 together. (Use a couple translations of the Bible if possible)

The Squire and the Scroll Coloring Book is also available. A lot of times children retain information better if they can do something with their hands while listening to a story. Particularly if your child is a tactile learner, the coloring book is a good investment.

SHEPHERDING A CHILD'S HEART

by Tedd Tripp

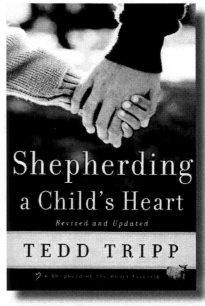

This wonderful book will teach you all about the most important thing you can do for your child: shepherd his or her heart. Tedd explains that every decision you make regarding your child—how you choose to discipline, which goals you decide to set for him or her, how you communicate with your child, etc.—should reflect the ultimate goal in life, which he believes is "to glorify God and enjoy Him forever" (56). Tedd explains that it is not helpful to focus on a child's behavior as something to examine and correct; the Bible tells us that all behavior stems from the heart, and it is the heart that we should be focusing on. We highly recommend this resource because if you can teach your child to examine the motives of his or her heart and guard his or her heart above anything, he or she will have the necessary tools to live a pure life.

POINTERS: We recommend this book for parents who have young children because it explains how to get to your child's heart. As we minister to thousands of parents every year, there is one thing we have learned about purity: More than a person's actions or philosophy, living a pure life is all about the state of a person's heart.

PREPARING HIM FOR THE OTHER WOMAN

by Sheri Rose Shepherd

When Sheri Rose was on vacation some years ago, her three-year-old son asked if she would marry him when he grew up. This question caused Sheri Rose to realize that as a mother, she only has a short time with her son, and that the training she gives him now has the potential to either help or hurt his marriage. What can you do to teach your son how to relate to his wife, provide for her needs, and become a Godly man? This quick and engaging read is packed with Biblical wisdom and practical ways to implement the advice in the book. This is an excellent resource for mothers of sons ages 3-19.

POINTER: At the end of every chapter, Sheri includes practical applications for mom to do with her son. These activities are tried and true, and will serve a mom well who is interested in putting the things she learned in the book into practice with her son.

Notes

Notes

1st Grade Intro

This grade features two intensive books on basic manners: *A Little Book of Manners for Girls* and *A Little Book of Manners for Boys*. This is a great age to focus on manners as your children are starting to become cognizant of people around them and how their actions affect others. Manners are integral to purity education because manners are essentially all about self control. Good manners teach people that they should check their behavior to ensure it is respectful and mindful of the people around them. If your children can grasp the basic principle behind good manners, they will be more inclined to practice self control in other areas of their lives, like sexuality. Maintaining purity in relationships with the opposite gender is really all about respecting the other person and practicing self control. Honing good manners is one of the building blocks that is going to help your children, not only in interacting in society, but also in maintaining pure relationships with the opposite gender.

Memory Verse
"For You formed my inward parts; You covered me in my mother's womb."
Psalm 139:13 (NKJV)

Godly Sexuality

Continue speaking to your children about how God made them and how He designed their bodies to function. Encourage your children to ask questions by having an appropriate reaction to their questions. Don't act annoyed or embarrassed by their inquiries, because this reaction will cause your children to associate negativity with the subject of sexuality. The truth is that God has created us in His image, and He has appointed mom and dad to teach their children about honoring the Lord with their bodies. Sometimes your children are going to surprise you, though. At these moments, when you are not sure what to answer, assure them you will think on their question and get back to them. Just remember to get back to them after you have time to consider your response!

Media Discernment

When I took my children to see the Veggie Tales™ movie, *Jonah*, there were some inappropriate previews that I did not want them to see. I was surprised because I figured *Jonah* would be safe entertainment for my children. I wasn't thinking about the previews before the movie. Therefore, I train my children on what they should do when these kinds of situations arise (or rather what not to do!). These situations are going to come up, so it's better that they know how to react instead of shielding them every time. At the movie during the preview, they closed their eyes and covered their ears. Also, another influence you should protect your child from is TV commercials. Especially if you watch sports programs, there are several ads that use promiscuity to help sell the products. At our house, we turn the TV off during the commercials, or at least mute the TV, especially if the commercials are inappropriate.

Spiritual Development

A lot of children have an innate sense that something is wrong, and it makes them feel uncomfortable. This uncomfortable feeling is actually their consciences at work. You can help your children listen to their God-given check system by talking through situations that make them feel uncomfortable.

Teachable Moments

When your child is exposed to inappropriate material, whether it's in a movie or on a magazine cover at the grocery store, make sure you address the issue with him or her. Don't just gloss over the situation when you know they saw it. Kids need to know when things they are seeing or witnessing are wrong. You don't need to go into incredible detail at this age, but it will serve your children well to know when the inappropriate things they are seeing are wrong. For instance, if they see a magazine in the grocery store where the cover model is inappropriately dressed, you might notice your son or daughter casting his or her eyes down quickly. You don't have to address the situation right then and there in the grocery store, but do address it, perhaps in the car on the way home. Ask your child "Did you notice that magazine in the checkout line? I did too. That lady was not wearing enough clothing, was she? Did that picture make you feel uncomfortable? You were right to feel uncomfortable because it's not right to let people see you with that little clothing on, is it?"

1st Grade Organizer

Tools for the Sandbox

- [ ] *Just Mom and Me Having Tea*
  by Mary J. Murray
- [ ] *A Little Book of Manners for Boys*
  by Bob and Emilie Barnes
- [ ] *A Little Book of Manners for Girls*
  by Emilie Barnes
- [ ] *Princess with a Purpose*
  by Kelly Chapman
- [ ] *A Warrior Prince for God*
  by Kelly Chapman
- [ ] *Will, God's Mighty Warrior*
  by Sheila Walsh
- [ ] *Why Do Birds Build Nests?*
  by Susan Horner
- [ ] *The Father Connection*
  by Josh McDowell
- [ ] *Project Blessing* (see page 11)
  by Kay and Julie Hiramine
- [ ] *Raising a Daughter after God's Own Heart*
  by Elizabeth George

Message in a Bottle

_____

_____

_____

_____

_____

_____

_____

_____

Lifeguard Watch - *Things your children should learn this year*

- [ ] Basic concept of how birds reproduce
- [ ] Basic concept of the seasons
- [ ] The pieces of the armor of God
- [ ] Table manners
- [ ] How to be a good sport
- [ ] How to be a good host or hostess
- [ ] How to share their toys
- [ ] How to behave at a social gathering
- [ ] How to greet other people politely
- [ ] God's Kingdom does not function like our culture
- [ ] Good character is more important than material things or circumstances in life
- [ ] What makes someone a prince or a princess
- [ ] They should always clarify with mom or dad the things they hear from their friends or siblings

Just Joining Us?

If this is your first year implementing the *Against the Tide* curriculum, there are a few resources we recommend starting with, before you jump into this year's resources:

- *The Wonderful Way Babies Are Made* (description on page 5)
- *The Story of Me* (description on page 18)
- *The Swimsuit Lesson* (description on page 6)
- *The Princess and the Kiss* (description on page 19)
- *The Squire and the Scroll* (description on page 21)
- *Guardians of Purity* (description on page 10)

Timeline Options

Option 1 – Week Study

Start each day by having your child repeat the memory verse back to you. Your goal is to have them saying the verse from memory by the end of the week.

Day 1: First half of *Why Do Birds Build Nests?*
Day 2: Second half of *Why Do Birds Build Nests?*
Day 3: *Will, God's Mighty Warrior*
Day 4: *A Little Book of Manners for Girls* and/or *A Little Book of Manners for Boys*
Day 5: *A Warrior Prince for God* and/or *Princess with a Purpose*

*The book *Just Mom and Me Having Tea* is a six-session study with week-long Bible study between the sessions. Since this resource cannot be completed in one week, we have left it out of the week study in order for you to fit it into another time in your year. You might find it most convenient to complete this study during the summer months.

Option 2 – Unit Study

Start each session by having your child recite the memory verse with you. Your goal is to have them saying the verse from memory by the end of the unit.

Week 1: *Why Do Birds Build Nests?*
Week 2: *Will, God's Mighty Warrior*
Week 3: *A Little Book of Manners for Girls* and/or *A Little Book of Manners for Boys*
Week 4: *A Warrior Prince for God* and/or *Princess with a Purpose*

*The book *Just Mom and Me Having Tea* is a six-session study with week-long Bible study between the sessions. Since this resource is slightly longer than the time for a unit study, we have left it out of the unit study in order for you to fit it into another time in your year. You might find it most convenient to complete this study during the summer months.

Option 3 – Family Devos

All of the children's books featured in this grade, with the exception of *Just Mom and Me Having Tea*, are appropriate to incorporate into your family devotions. Especially with *Why Do Birds Build Nests*, this is an excellent book to share with your family during devotion time. It does not specifically address reproduction for people; the author has done an excellent job giving the creation science behind how birds reproduce. It explains reproduction and creation from a shameless perspective. As far as *Just Mom and Me Having Tea* is concerned, there may be concepts or principles you may want to share in your family devotions, but this study is best done one-on-one with mom and daughter. Be sure to recite your memory verse at the beginning or end of your family devotion time.

WHY DO BIRDS BUILD NESTS?

by Susan Horner

This is the second book in the *Miracle of Creation Series*. This book follows birds and outlines their reproduction as they instinctively follow the seasons—thereby following God's timing. It's a wonderful example of how God created living things to reproduce. Also included in the back of this book are several family activities designed to increase your child's understanding of reproduction and also the virtues associated with following God's timing.

The author, Susan Horner, suggests interspersing the activities she provides in the back of the book throughout the reading. The activities provide real-life examples of the information in the book.

DISCUSSION QUESTIONS

From the Family Fun Activities in the back of the book:
Set up a birdbath. Birds enjoy taking baths and need to drink water every day. Be sure to clean and refill your birdbath with fresh water at least every other day. A bird scout will see it and tell other birds. Soon your birdbath will be a wildlife hangout. Find more activities on page 28.

What are the four seasons?

How did God create people and birds to be similar?

Can you think of other things that follow seasons?

What season are we in right now? What are the birds doing in this season?

WILL GOD'S MIGHTY WARRIOR

by Sheila Walsh

A young boy like Will can easily find adventure around every corner. Whether it's leaping tall buildings made out of blocks or saving his sister from his dog Ralph, Will is on the job. However, it's not until he receives a lesson from his father about the armor of God that Will finds his true calling as God's Mighty Warrior. This delightful story will stir your son's God-given desire to be a warrior in His army.

will
God's Mighty Warrior

Sheila Walsh
Illustrated by Meredith Johnson

POINTER: Much like girls appreciate being princesses, boys desire to be warriors. In their own ways, every boy has a natural desire to protect, to serve, and to live his life for a worthy calling. This book does an excellent job of highlighting and encouraging this desire in an appropriate way. You can shape your son's character by giving him examples of warriors in the Bible and throughout history who lived by a sacred code and left their societies better for having hosted them.

DISCUSSION QUESTIONS

Because Will learns about the armor of God in this story, help your child to look up and then read about it in the Bible (Ephesians 6:11-17).

How can you use the Sword of the Spirit?

Do you remember all the pieces that make up the armor of God? What are they?

Do you want to be one of God's Mighty Warriors?

How do you think following God is like being in His army?

A Little Book of Manners:
Courtesy & Kindness for Young Ladies

by Emilie Barnes

This charming book is packed with lessons for your little girl that are designed to teach her how to become a polite and attentive young lady. The lessons teach her how to introduce herself to someone, how to behave at a friend's house, how to take a phone message, how to communicate to others, and much more. Help your daughter build a Godly character as she learns to conduct herself respectfully around other people.

In addition to reading this book, you can also pull it out as situations arise where your daughter might need to refine her manners.

Activities & Discussion Points

Can you give me an example of how NOT to behave at a party?

What are some ways you can work on having good manners?

Why are manners important?

Dennis and Barbara Rainey hold a "Manner's Week" frequently in their house, where they make a concerted effort to practice good manners. The Raineys do things like making sure the boys hold the doors open for the women of the family, pull chairs out for other people, etc., while the girls practice behaving modestly and speaking politely to one another during the special week. This is a wonderful idea for children of all ages, and you can highlight this book in your child's curriculum during your week devoted to manners.

A Little Book of Manners for Boys

by Bob & Emilie Barnes

This is a wonderful book designed to teach your little boy how to be a young gentleman. This entertaining book touches on issues all little boys sometimes need help with: watching his language, speaking to elders, taking care of his belongings, being a good sport, being a good leader and friend, treating girls respectfully, and much more! Also included is a short section on the importance of manners, to help your son see the relationship between practicing good manners and emulating Godly character.

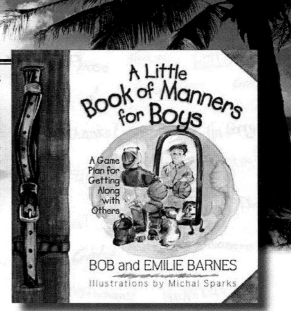

In addition to reading this book together, you can also consult it when situations arise where your young gentleman may need to refine his manners a bit.

Activities & Discussion Points

Can you give me an example of how NOT to behave when you are playing a game?

After reading this book, can you notice areas where you can improve your manners?

Why are manners important?

Dennis and Barbara Rainey of FamilyLife hold a "Manner's Week" frequently in their house, where they make a concerted effort to practice good manners. The Raineys do things like making sure the boys hold the doors open for the women of the family, pull chairs out for other people, etc., while the girls practice behaving modestly and speaking politely to one another during the special week. This is a wonderful idea for children of all ages, and you can highlight this book in your child's curriculum during your week devoted to manners.

PRINCESS WITH A PURPOSE *(for girls)*

by Kelly Chapman

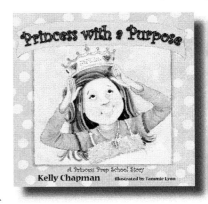

Caroline has always wanted to be a princess, but she's afraid the circumstances of her life don't allow her to qualify as a princess. She doesn't live in a castle, have servants, or even a father to call her own. Imagine her surprise, however, when she learns that you don't need any of those things to be a princess. She has a Father in Heaven who desires to be her Savior and Provider. Teach your daughter about the nature of a true princess with this charming tale.

POINTER: This book does an excellent job explaining to girls that no matter their circumstance—whether they are poor or rich, have one parent or two—they are children of the Heavenly King, and that is a very important position!

Why did Caroline think she couldn't be a princess at the beginning of the story? What made her change her mind?

How do you treat your siblings?

How did Caroline treat her sister, Kendall, in the story?

What did Caroline learn about becoming a princess? (Look up Romans 8:16-18)

What makes someone beautiful?

DISCUSSION QUESTIONS

A WARRIOR PRINCE FOR GOD *(for boys)*

by Kelly Chapman

Luke is having a hard time on his baseball team. After being the last one at bat and striking out, his spirits are low. But after a vivid dream where he goes to the Warrior Academy, he learns that he can be brave and courageous when the Lord is at his side. He learns that even in the tough situations—when he feels down and insignificant—the fact that he has chosen Jesus as his Savior and commits to serve Him makes Luke a warrior prince. And a warrior prince for God is no small thing.

POINTER: Luke learns in this story that he doesn't have to be tough or cool, like the twins in the story, to serve God. Use this story to explain to your son that true courage and bravery comes from God, and we are strongest when we rely on the Lord.

Why did Drakon retreat after Luke mentioned Jesus' name? (Look up Philippians 2:9-11)

Who does Drakon represent?

Why did Drakon the snake claim to be Luke's friend?

Has anyone criticized you before for doing something well?

How do you become a warrior prince for God?

DISCUSSION QUESTIONS

Just Mom and Me Having Tea
(for girls)

by Mary J. Murray

This is an awesome resource for you and your daughter to enjoy together. So far, I have used this resource with my three oldest girls and they all enjoyed the quality time with Mom. This book includes creative crafts you and your daughter can make together and also timeless values taught through light-hearted stories and insightful questions. The focus of this study is to teach daily devotion and Bible study. This book will help you and your daughter get in the habit of learning about the Lord and His Word together. This is one of many great resources designed to strengthen the bond between the two of you, so that when she gets older she will feel comfortable coming to you with whatever is on her heart.

Just Mom and Me Having Tea is all about learning how to study your Bible and pray everyday. Between the tea sessions, your daughter will have short, daily Bible study.

Before you start *Just Mom and Me Having Tea,* read through the craft sections and make a list of the materials you will need. Give yourself a little time to collect or purchase these items to have available when you want to start. That way you won't have to postpone or interrupt your mother-daughter time to find materials.

The Father Connection
by Josh McDowell

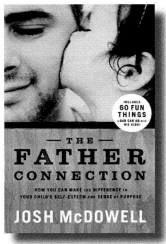

Josh McDowell has been a Christian leader for a number of years now, but his first ministry has been fathering his children. In this encouraging book for dads, Josh highlights ten character traits that make a father a pertinent and healthy influence in his children's lives. Now more than ever, fathers are needed in the very center of their families' lives. Yet some dads miss the importance of their role, and the lack results in children who are constantly seeking approval and attention in destructive ways. Learn how to father like the Heavenly Father in Josh McDowell's quick read. You will never see your role the same way again, Dad!

The strong point of *The Father Connection* is its straightforward instruction and ideas. It answers the question "How can I be a good dad?" in a positive way. Included at the end of this book are 60 fun things dad can do with his kids, which makes it easy for dad to start right away being a positive role model and coach for his children.

Elizabeth George writes to mothers who have daughters all ages about the practical tips that will help them raise a girl who follows God with all her heart. Covering the basics of mentoring your daughter and modeling a life submitted to Christ, Elizabeth gives encouragement to mothers who truly want the best for their daughters. Integral to her advice is praying for your daughter over her specific prayer needs. This is an all-around good book on how to be the best influence you can be on your daughter.

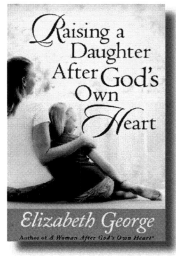

Included in this book are "Mom's Think Pad" sections following each chapter. These include excellent questions and scripture study to help you process the words in Elizabeth's book. Don't pass these sections up - they are incredibly helpful!

Notes

2nd Grade Intro

The age range from 6-12 is a pivotal time in your child's life. During these years, your child will look to you for understanding and encouragement in all areas of his or her life. It is vital that you protect his innocence as much as you possibly can and teach him the importance of coming to you with his questions and concerns. Also, if you have boys, this is a great age to begin instilling the necessity of manners—especially toward girls and elders—so that he can understand the importance of behaving like a gentleman. For girls also, this is an excellent age to begin instilling the values a modest, ladylike girl possesses.

Memory Verse
"Create in me a clean heart, O God, And renew a steadfast spirit within me."
Psalm 51:10 (NKJV)

Points

FOR 2ND GRADE

GODLY SEXUALITY

This year, we feature *The Wonderful Way Babies Are Made*, one of our favorite books about the beauty of God's creation. We can't stress how important it is to instill in your children a healthy and truthful sense of the nature of sexuality the way God designed it. Our culture is so set on presenting sex and sexuality as something wrong and disgraceful. But we as parents need to be diligent to teach them about appropriate sexuality; it is beautiful in God's timing and it's something that should be honored in its appropriate time.

There is a difference between innocence and ignorance. To teach your children the truth about sex and God's purpose for sexuality does not ruin their innocence. It does shatter their ignorance, which is what they will learn from the culture if we are silent on the subject.

SPIRITUAL DEVELOPMENT

It's important for your children to know that the rules you and your spouse enforce come from the Bible. They need to know what God's word says about honoring one's parents, obeying authority, telling the truth, etc. This tactic has two purposes: first of all, it shows your children that you are deferring to God's authority as far as rules are concerned, and it also shows them that we have rules for a reason. God knew we needed rules for our own good and safety. He never puts a rule in His book without a reason that is for our own good. These are principles your children will benefit from knowing at this young age.

MEDIA DISCERNMENT

As your children get older, they will have more opportunity to spend time at friends' houses. Even if your family is close to other families, establish clear boundaries with your children about what is ok for them to watch or play at their friends' houses. Also, be conscious of the influence of siblings in the friend's house. Sometimes we don't realize that the friend might be ok, but older siblings may be up to no good on computers, etc. One thing you can do is communicate your family's boundaries to your child's friend's parents so everyone is on the same page.

TEACHABLE MOMENTS

Manners are something that should be an ongoing lesson with your children. While we didn't include any books on manners in this grade, take every opportunity that comes up to instruct your children about how they can practice good manners. Don't look for situations to humiliate or reprimand your children in front of strangers, but if there is a situation where they could have behaved differently, be sure to point these times out to them. Point out where their behavior was not appropriate or polite, and then ask them how they could have handled the situation differently.

2ND GRADE ORGANIZER

Tools for the Sandbox

- [ ] *The Brave Young Knight*
      by Karen Kingsbury
- [ ] *Everyday Graces*
      edited by Karen Santorum
- [ ] *God's Mighty Warrior Devotional Bible*
      by Sheila Walsh
- [ ] *Lady in Waiting for Little Girls*
      by Jackie Kendall and Dede Kendall
- [ ] *The Princess and the Three Knights*
      by Karen Kingsbury
- [ ] *Princess Parable Series*
      by Jeanna Young & Jacqueline Johnson
- [ ] *The Wonderful Way Babies Are Made*
      by Larry Christenson
- [ ] *Loving Our Kids on Purpose*
      by Danny Silk
- [ ] *Project Blessing* (see page 11)
      by Kay and Julie Hiramine

Message in a Bottle

_____

_____

_____

_____

_____

_____

_____

Lifeguard Watch - *Things your children should learn this year*

- [ ] All the pieces of the armor of God
- [ ] Love is patient
- [ ] God designed all living things to reproduce in a similar way
- [ ] It is important to treat other people with respect
- [ ] Table manners
- [ ] How to guard their tongues
- [ ] A princess is a daughter of the Heavenly King
- [ ] What makes someone brave
- [ ] Basic concept of how babies are made
- [ ] Understanding of what adoption is

Just Joining Us?

If this is your first year doing the *Against the Tide* curriculum, there are a few resources we recommend starting with, before you jump into this year's resources:

- *The Story of Me* (description on page 18)
- *The Swimsuit Lesson* (description on page 6)
- *The Princess and the Kiss* (description on page 19)
- *The Squire and the Scroll* (description on page 21)
- *Guardians of Purity* (description on page 10)

TIMELINE OPTIONS

Option 1 — Week Study

Start each day by having your child repeat the memory verse back to you. Your goal is to have them saying the verse from memory by the end of the week.

Day 1: *The Princess and the Three Knights* and/or *The Brave Young Knight*
Day 2: *The Wonderful Way Babies Are Made* and/or a book from the *Princess Parable Series*
Day 3: *Everyday Graces** (Note: pick a longer story on this day) and/or a book from the *Princess Parable Series*
Day 4: *God's Mighty Warrior Devotional Bible** and/or *Lady in Waiting for Little Girls** and *Everyday Graces*
Day 5: repeat Day 4

*These resources will take you longer to get through than the week-long study allows for. We recommend starting these books during the week study and continuing through the school year with them. *Everyday Graces* is a collection of poems, short stories, and excerpts from chapter books that you can read at a leisurely pace. It's an excellent book to share around the lunch or dinner table with the whole family. *Will God's Mighty Warrior Devotional Bible* is not set up in chapters or sessions, so you can move through this book as you see fit; perhaps you can implement a few pages at bedtime each night. Finally, *Lady in Waiting for Little Girls* includes a preface lesson and then 10 lessons. The lessons are not long, making it possible for you to get through at least two lessons during the week long study, and then you will have 9 lessons left to integrate into the rest of your school year or summer.

Option 2 — Unit Study

Start each session by having your child recite the memory verse with you. Your goal is to have them saying the verse from memory by the end of the unit.

Week 1: *The Brave Young Knight* and/or *The Princess and the Three Knights*, 3 lessons from *Lady in Waiting for Little Girls* and/or pages 2-37 of *God's Mighty Warrior Devotional Bible**
Week 2: *The Wonderful Way Babies Are Made*, 2 lessons from *Lady in Waiting for Little Girls*, a book from the *Princess Parable Series*, and/or pages 38-73 of *God's Mighty Warrior Devotional Bible*
Week 3: The first section of *Everyday Graces*** ("Good Manners at Home"), 3 lessons from *Lady in Waiting for Little Girls*, a book from the *Princess Parable Series*, and/or 74-109 pages of *God's Mighty Warrior Devotional Bible*
Week 4: The second section of *Everyday Graces* ("Using Words Wisely"), 3 lessons from *Lady in Waiting for Little Girls* and/or pages 110-145 of *God's Mighty Warrior Devotional Bible*

*This unit study will take you through the first 145 pages of *God's Mighty Warrior Devotional Bible*. You will have 169 pages left after the unit study is complete.
**This unit study will take you through the first two sections of *Everyday Graces*, but the book is too lengthy to finish in one unit. This is an easy one to implement into other family times, however, and can even be a welcome addition to lunch-time or dinner conversation.

Option 3 — Family Devos

Be sure to recite your memory verse at the beginning or end of your family devotion time. The following books can be incorporated into your regular family devotion times:

Everyday Graces
The Princess and the Three Knights (even though this book is geared toward girls, its message about the nature of true love applies to both girls and boys)
The Brave Young Knight (even though this book is geared toward boys, its message about the value of good character is great for boys and girls)
God's Mighty Warrior Devotional Bible (this one is also geared toward boys, but contains lessons that apply to both genders.)
The Princess Parable Series

The other books featured in 2nd grade, *The Wonderful Way Babies Are Made* and *Lady in Waiting for Little Girls*, are typically better received when read one-on-one. However, if you have all girls and want to incorporate *Lady in Waiting for Little Girls* into your family devotion time, it would make an excellent addition to your family study. You can also use discretion with *The Wonderful Way Babies Are Made*. Some families with children close in age have incorporated this book in their family devotions without issue, but please evaluate if this would be best for your family.

The Wonderful Way Babies Are Made

by Larry Christenson

This is a wonderful book for kids 3-10. The big text is for younger kids, while the text in the boxes should be saved for older, more mature kids. Each set of text communicates the wonder of God's creation as it tells the story of how God created the world, how He made plants, animals, people, and families, and the wonderful way He makes babies. We love this book because it gives children a Godly, positive perspective on creation and life in general. It also has a profound section on adoption and explains how Jesus was adopted by Joseph and Mary.

Pointers

Read with your child the big text (NOT in the boxes). If your child is a good reader and you are concerned about him or her reading the text in the boxes over your shoulder, sit around a table, where you can read the big text and then show the pictures. Also, if there are pictures in this book that you don't want your child to see, you can also employ the sitting around the table method, showing only the pictures you want to show. Make sure to read the text on every page, though, even if you choose to skip the pictures. Be sure to put this book in a secure place if your children are used to perusing any book on your book shelves (like mine are).

Discussion Questions

After you and your child read this book, have him or her write responses to some topics based on the book. Discuss your child's answers with him or her. A few examples include:

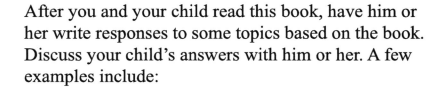

> *Write a letter to God telling Him how great you think His creation is. Be sure to thank Him for making you so special.*

> *Write down things that you feel are special about the way God makes babies.*

Everyday Graces

edited by Karen Santorum

This is an excellent resource for a wide age range of children. Teach your children the value of manners as you read them poems and stories about manners and people who either emulated them, or did not. The material consists of excerpts from *Anne of Green Gables* and *The Chronicles of Narnia*, among other stories from both classic and modern literature. This is a great book to use while the family's sitting down to dinner, getting tucked in for bed, or just in need of some instruction! Included in this book are tidbits about how each story or poem relates to manners. This is a fun, easy-to-implement way to teach your children all about the behavior necessary to treat others with respect and be respected themselves.

Although the book is rather large, my family was able to get through it pretty quickly by reading it at lunch time. My kids liked this book so much, they were always asking to read it. Your children are sure to love all the stories and poems in this book.

Discussion Questions

Did the main character of the story/poem practice good manners? Why or why not?

If they did not practice good manners, how could they have behaved better?

Do you always practice good manners? Think of a time when you behaved the right way. How did you know you were doing the right thing?

Now think of a time when you have not practiced good manners. How could you have behaved differently that would have been better?

BOOKS NOT TO MISS for Boys

THE BRAVE YOUNG KNIGHT
by Karen Kingsbury

A young knight from the west side of the kingdom is strong, smart, and fast. But above all these things, he is caring and kind. When the King announces that the bravest knight in all the kingdom will be named price, the young knight from the west village knows he should try to win this honorable position. After training the best way he knows how, the young knight is ready to be tested. Among the knights from the other kingdoms, he doesn't feel like the best. But the young knight learns that sometimes the winner isn't necessarily the strongest or fastest or most intelligent - the winner is the one with the best character.

DISCUSSION QUESTIONS

Why did the young knight play with the boy who couldn't walk and help the lady carry her bricks?

What made the young knight different from the other knights who were taking the test?

Read 1 Samuel 16:1-13, the story about God choosing David to be king of Israel. Why do you think God chose David? What was David's character like?

Do you think God will bless you for being honest and integrous like He did the brave young knight? Find a scripture to prove your opinion.

GOD'S MIGHTY WARRIOR DEVOTIONAL BIBLE
by Sheila Walsh

Going through the armor of God in an engaging way, this devotional is jam-packed with scripture, succinct lessons, and fun activities. Your son will love learning how to be God's Mighty Warrior as he learns valuable lessons like how to use scripture in tough situations, how to turn the other cheek when he is hurt or offended, and how to trust in God.

POINTER:

This devotional uses the *International Children's Bible*. Even if this isn't your preferred translation, a lot of times children gain understanding when they read multiple translations. A certain version might use words or phrasing that simply make more sense to them than others. If there is a certain version of the Bible you prefer over this *International Children's Bible*, consider reading both.

In addition to the activities and discussion questions throughout this devotional, another idea is to have your son recite the armor of God when you read this book.

DISCUSSION QUESTIONS

Books Not To Miss for Girls

The Princess and the Three Knights
by Karen Kingsbury

This is a beautifully-illustrated medieval times tale about the nature of true love. The story highlights the fact that true love protects always, no matter the situation. The young princess in this story has a heart of gold that many are attracted to, but only the knight who passes the wise king's tests will win her hand in marriage. But these tests aren't like other tests the knights have faced before. To pass these tests, the brave knights must understand the nature of true love.

Pointer:

Don't be surprised if this book becomes an instant favorite in your home. You may end up reading it a few times in a day. But don't be annoyed; a lot of times children like to mull over stories, especially if they have a deep meaning. If they are asking to hear a story over and over again, it's because they are trying to process its full meaning.

Discussion Questions

Why do you think the people of the kingdom thought the princess was beautiful on the inside? What makes someone beautiful on the inside?

What did this story teach you about love? What is one of the characteristics of love?

Why did the king let the third knight marry his daughter?

What do you think the three knights' motives were to marry the princess? In other words, what made them want to marry the princess? (If your child doesn't know what the word motive means, look it up in a dictionary for children)

Look up 1 Corinthians 13:4+5. Based on these verses, do you think the two knights who did not marry the princess really loved her? Why or why not?

Lady in Waiting for Little Girls
by Jackie Kendall and Dede Kendall

This mother-daughter study focuses on 10 spiritual choices every young princess should make. These choices include obeying God, relying on God for salvation, being content, and more. Each lesson includes real-life stories, discussion questions and activities, and stories of women in the Bible who have made these same choices in their efforts to serve God. While choosing to obey God in everything isn't always easy, Jackie and Dede want to show girls that no matter what their situation, they have the ability to obey God because they have been called by His name, and He is with them to encourage and guide them through their lives.

Pointer:

As discussed in the introduction to *Lady in Waiting for Little Girls,* Jackie and Dede suggest taking one lesson a week. The authors have also included a "Princess Quiz" before the 10 lessons, which is designed to gauge how your little lady in waiting is doing in her walk with the Lord, and determine areas where she can walk more closely with her King.

Princess Parables

by Jeanna Young & Jacqueline Johnson

Using parables Jesus told, these charming princess stories follow sisters Grace, Joy, Hope, Charity, and Faith. Young readers will love the endearing stories and also learn quite a bit about the nature of God's Kingdom and His extravagent love for us. Pick a specific parable or two to focus on, or enjoy all 5.

Princess Joy's Birthday Blessing
(The Wedding Feast)

Princess Faith's Mysterious Garden
(The Parable of the Sower)

Princess Hope and the Hidden Treasure
(The Pearl of Great Price)

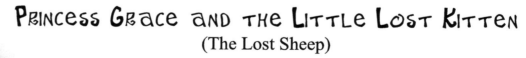

Princess Charity's Courageous Heart
(The Good Samaritan)

Princess Grace and the Little Lost Kitten
(The Lost Sheep)

Discussion Questions

Which parable from the Bible is this story based on? Did the story help you understand the parable better?

Look up the word parable in the dictionary. In your own words, what does it mean?

What lesson did the main character of the story learn?

LOVING OUR KIDS ON PURPOSE

by Danny Silk

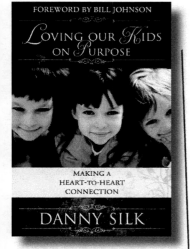

Loving Our Kids on Purpose shows you how to plant in your children the principles of the Kingdom of God and a heart for the Lord. Unlike other books on discipline, Danny Silk gets to the heart of training children to fear God and honor their parents. Eliminating the tool of punishment is key to his unique approach. He trains parents to allow their children to learn and make mistakes while the stakes are lower - while they are still under the protection and guidance of their parents. It's not always the easiest approach to training children, but in the end, children learn where their God-given boundaries are and how to make wise decisions. Danny's philosophy is all about equipping children to one day be self-sustaining, responsible adults.

Even if discipline has not been a major issue for your children, this book has helpful information and practical application for every family and situation.

Notes

Notes

3rd Grade
Intro

As your children move into older grades, we suggest having them write out their answers to discussion questions as well as talk to you about them. Not only will this exercise give them practice in writing and reading comprehension, it will also help reinforce the lessons they are learning.

Memory Verse
"Who shall ascend into the hill of the Lord? or who shall stand in his holy place? He that hath clean hands, and a pure heart; who hath not lifted up his soul unto vanity, nor sworn deceitfully." Psalm 24:3-4

Media Discernment

The world's bent is to make our children grow up too fast and to burden them with false messages about God, their sexuality, and the world. This trend is noticeable in cartoons or "kids' movies". More often than not, these cartoons include adult subjects and humor that goes over our children's heads, but still affects them negatively. Soon they are desensitized to these messages and start not to notice when they come up. This is why it is so important to review all of the media they consume—movies, television, books, magazines, music, etc. We can no longer assume that just because something is advertised as being "kid friendly" it is actually appropriate for our children. Especially at this age, children are very much into books. Be sure to review the books they are reading before they get their hands on them. Sometimes we pass books off our radar because they seem harmless, but we need to be diligent about monitoring this influence as well.

Spiritual Development

It has been said by child psychologists that the ages 8-12 are conviction shaping ages, while the teen years are conviction testing ages. As your children mature through this stage, keep in mind that the example they are witnessing from you and your spouse is shaping their convictions about how to relate to other people, how to handle problems, and what is most important in life. Also, be sure to monitor the influences coming from peers, acquaintances, and even other family members. While you can't ensure your children are always around people setting a Godly example, you can address improper behavior they may be exposed to. Your comments don't have to be judgmental, but the point is to let your children know what is appropriate and what is not.

Godly Sexuality

This year we feature the book *Before I Was Born*, which explains, in simple and discreet terms, what sex is. As with all of the resources we suggest throughout this curriculum, mom and dad should judge when it is best to share this information with their children. While every child is different, it has been our experience that for mom and dad to be the first ones to explain what sex is, we need to have these discussions sooner rather than later.

Teachable Moments

While on a family vacation to Mexico, my family and I had the misfortune of riding in a boat with a handful of severely inebriated college students. One young lady was so disoriented, I was surprised she even made it onto the boat. My poor husband got to sit right next to her, which made him nervous he was going to end up with the contents of this girl's stomach all over his shoes. Sitting there, huddled with my five children, ranging in age from 2 to 15, I was a little nervous about the impact this scene was having my young ones. Instead of brushing the incident off, though, I used it as a good opportunity to express some clear expectations. I made sure my children knew that I NEVER wanted to see them doing anything like this. I think they were all pretty shocked, but they got the message: Drunk people do embarrassing, crazy, and dangerous things. Being drunk is not good. I waited until we were off the boat, out of earshot of the college students, because I wanted my children to feel comfortable talking to me about the situation.

3RD GRADE ORGANIZER

Tools for the Sandbox

- ☐ *Before I Was Born*
  by Carolyn Nystrom

- ☐ *Character Building from the Life of Jesus*
  by V. Gilbert Beers

- ☐ *Knights, Maidens, & Dragons*
  by Julia Duin

- ☐ *88 Great Daddy-Daughter Dates*
  by Rob & Joanna Teigen

- ☐ *Beautifully Made! Series*
  edited by Julie Hiramine

- ☐ *Project Blessing* (see page 11)
  by Kay and Julie Hiramine

- ☐ *Secure Daughters, Confident Sons*
  by Glenn T. Stanton

Message in a Bottle

_____

_____

_____

_____

_____

_____

_____

Lifeguard Watch - *Things your children should learn this year*

- ☐ True love is worth waiting for
- ☐ God designed sex for marriage
- ☐ Basic concept of what sex is
- ☐ Basic concept of how their bodies are going to start changing
- ☐ What makes people honorable or good is their character

- ☐ You can use God's Word to fight temptation and make good choices
- ☐ Christ is our example of good character
- ☐ Character is more important than appearances or your position in life

Just Joining Us?

If this is your first year doing the *Against the Tide* curriculum, there are a few resources we recommend starting with, before you jump into this year's resources:

- *The Wonderful Way Babies Are Made* (description on page 41)
- *The Princess and the Kiss* (description on page 19)
- *The Squire and the Scroll* (description on page 21)
- *Guardians of Purity* (description on page 10)

TIMELINE OPTIONS

Option 1 – *Week Study*

Start each day by having your child repeat the memory verse back to you. Your goal is to have them saying the verse from memory by the end of the week.

- Day 1: *Before I Was Born*
- Day 2: 2 stories from *Knights, Maidens and Dragons*
- Day 3: 2 stories from *Knights, Maidens and Dragons*
- Day 4: 2 stories from *Knights, Maidens and Dragons*
- Day 5: First lesson in *Character Builidng from the Life of Jesus** and *Beautifully Made*! (optional - please read the description for this book)

Character Building from the Life of Jesus will take you longer than one week to complete. We have started you off with one lesson during the week study, and then you will have 59 more lessons to complete throughout the rest of your school year or summer.

Option 2 – *Unit Study*

Start each session by having your child recite the memory verse with you. Your goal is to have them saying the verse from memory by the end of the unit.

Week 1: *Before I Was Born* and 4 lessons from *Character Building from the Life of Jesus**
Week 2: 2 stories from *Knights Maidens and Dragons* and 4 lessons from *Character Building from the Life of Jesus*
Week 3: 2 stories from *Knights Maidens and Dragons* and 4 lessons from *Character Building from the Life of Jesus*
Week 4: 2 stories from *Knights Maidens and Dragons*, 4 lessons from *Character Building from the Life of Jesus* and *Beautifully Made*! (optional - please see description for this book)

*This unit study will take you through 16 lessons from *Character Building from the Life of Jesus*. This book features 60 lessons, so you will have 44 lessons left after finishing this unit study.

Option 3 – *Family Devos*

Be sure to recite your memory verse at the beginning or end of your family devotion time.

The following children's books are appropriate to incorporate into your family's regular devotional time:
  Knights, Maidens and Dragons
  Character Building from the Life of Jesus

Because *Beautifully Made!* is designed to be one-on-one for mom and daughter, we don't recommend incorporating this series into your devotion times.

Before I Was Born should be handled with discretion because it is a book that discusses issues of sexuality. We have found that for most family situations, it does best as a one-on-one between parent and child.

Before I Was Born

by Carolyn Nystrom

This is the second book in the *God's Design for Sex Series*. Your children will love the pictures and simple style Nystrom used to write this book. It covers differences between girls and boys, some changes to expect while maturing, and the basic facts about sex, all from a Biblical perspective. This is a great book your children will love to read with you as they discover God's design for their bodies and lives.

The suggested ages on the cover of this book are 5-8. While these ages are appropriate for some families, we have included *Before I Was Born* in third grade, on the older side of this age suggestion. It has been our experience that for most families, third grade is best. As with any of the resources we recommend, however, parents should evaluate when it is appropriate to share with their children.

Discussion Questions

> *Look up Psalm 139:14.*
> *What does this verse teach you about your body?*

Are you looking forward to being grown up? What are some things you are looking forward to doing as a grown up?

God designed your body to grow up and change. What are some changes you've noticed so far?

CHARACTER BUILDING FROM THE LIFE OF JESUS

by V. Gilbert Beers

This wonderful book features 60 stories from the Bible about Jesus and the principles He taught. Each story highlights a different character trait that Jesus portrayed: things like helpfulness, patience, belonging, purpose, obedience, and faith. Your children will not only learn about the witness and character of our Lord, the author also helps them to apply the teaching to their own lives - helping them to see how they can practice all the good things Jesus taught us. Coupled with dramatic illustrations and comments on the scripture, this book will have your kids asking to read it over and over!

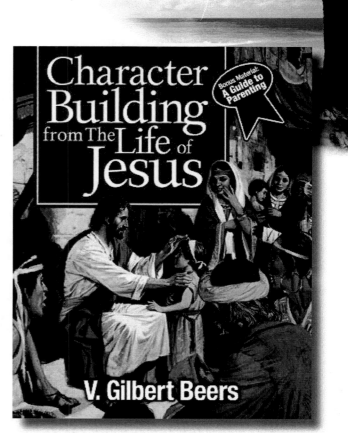

Included in the back of this book is "A Guide to Parenting". Be sure to read this section - it contains many valuable pearls of wisdom that will aid you in teaching your children about Godly character.

This book makes an excellent family devotion study - its keen insights into scripture, combined with facts about Jewish life make it engaging for a wide variety of ages.

You can read this book cover to cover like a chapter book, or if you look in the back, the author has organized a daily study guide for each of the 60 stories.

KNIGHTS, MAIDENS AND DRAGONS

by Julia Duin

Knights, Maidens and Dragons is a compilation of six allegorical tales relating to purity. The stories are set in six different places around the world, all from the medieval time period. The characters are both male and female, and the morals of these stories range from patience, to faithfulness, to service to the King. My family loves this book so much that we read the entire thing once every year. These stories are gems.

While we have included *Knights, Maidens and Dragons* in third grade, since the stories are parables, they can be read to many different ages. This is an excellent book to share around the dinner table, during family devotions, or at bedtime. It never fails to amaze me how much my children understand the deep messages in these stories. They truly are great pieces of literature.

DISCUSSION QUESTIONS

Waiting for True Love

Do you understand that the way in which the three girls made their cloaks reflected the way they chose their husbands?

Do you feel sorry that Christina and Felicity's hearts were broken and they did not marry their one true love?

For Parents: What did Sylvester do correctly?

Tell me a little about the three girls' characters. How do their characters influence their outcomes?

What do you think Christopher and Felix should have done differently to help their daughters succeed?

In the Desert of Waiting

What do you think Shapur learned from his test of manhood?

Shapur would rather wait with his camel than continue on to the city of desire. What does this say about his character? Can you think of a word to describe his action?

What does this story have to do with purity and waiting for true love?

How is Shapur different from his cousins?

DISCUSSION QUESTIONS

Ederyn's Promise

Obviously, not everyone got to serve the king, so how was Ederyn different from other people?

What did he have that other people did not?

Why do you think Ederyn persevered the way he did?

How does this relate to purity?

The Enchanted Necklace

Why did the prince say he would willingly drink from Olga's hands? What characteristics does Olga have that the prince admires? How does Olga later lose these qualities?

Why is it significant that black nighthawks and black bats hovered around Olga when she commanded the beads to make her a pretty dress?

The theme of sacrifice is prevalent throughout this story. What can we learn about purity from sacrifice? What kind of sacrifices can you think of that Jesus performed in order for us to live pure lives?

The Jester's Sword

Why is it significant that Aldebaran gets his inspiration from stars? Do you think it is foolish or admirable that Aldebaran gets his inspiration from something so majestic and so far away?

What important lesson does Aldebaran learn about being humble?

Consider Vesta for a moment. Do you feel sorry that she waited her whole life to marry Aldebaran, but never sees him alive again? Do you think it is admirable the way she waits for him? What does her faithfulness express about Godly relationships?

Princess Winsome and the Jade Dragon

Look up the words wisdom and winsome. How do these definitions compare to Princess Winsome's and Prince Wisdom's characters? How are these words and their characters different?

What does this story teach us about how a gentleman should act toward a lady? What lessons can we learn from the warrior's character?

In this story, the girl was pursued by the warrior. Is this the way God designed relationships between people who are going to be married?

Beautifully Made! Series *(for girls)*

edited by Julie Hiramine

Beautifully Made is a three-book series designed to guide girls and their mothers through the transition from girlhood to womanhood. These books specifically talk about body changes and starting your first period. The first book, *Approaching Womanhood*, is for moms and their daughters to read together, before the start of the daughter's first period. Book 2, *Celebrating Womanhood*, is for the daughter when she starts her first period, and Book 3, *Wisdom from a Woman*, is just for mom to read. In this grade, we recommend using books 1 and 3.

Approaching Womanhood (Book 1)

Approaching Womanhood gives age-appropriate information about maturing into womanhood from a positive and Godly perspective. Your daughter will find easy-to-understand discussion on body changes, menstruation, and maturing into womanhood. *Approaching Womanhood* is designed for mother and daughter to go through together and helps to make the transition into womanhood a less anxious time. If your daughter is an early bloomer, read the first half of this book and whatever you feel is appropriate in the second half with her. It is a good idea that you and your daughter read this book before she starts her period so that she is comfortable with the concept by the time she starts.

After your daughter reads this book, sit down and ask her some questions related to the material. (A mother-daughter activity would be most appropriate)

> *Why do you think God made women's bodies this way?*

> *Have you ever heard of someone talking about her period? What have you heard that makes you anxious? Would you like to talk to me about your period? Are you nervous about any body changes?*

Wisdom from a Woman (Book 3)

The third book in the *Beautifully Made! Series*, this is a book of hope and encouragement for mom. In addition to information about hormones and biology, mom will also find several stories from mothers about some of the discussions they had with their daughters. You will also find sound advice to mothers about how and when to tell your daughter about menstrual cycles and body changes and how to make it a positive transition for your little girl.

We suggest you read this book now, even if you haven't gone through *Approaching Womanhood* with your daughter yet, as this book will help you prepare for the special time your daughter is approaching. Also, if you decide to share *Approaching Womanhood* with your daughter this year, be sure to read *Wisdom from a Woman* first, as there are several good ideas for mom to share with her daughter.

Secure Daughters, Confident Sons

by Glenn T. Stanton

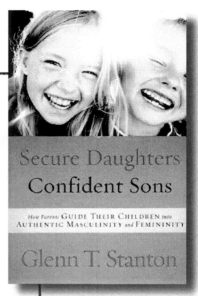

Exploring the issue of gender differences in various cultures, as well as applying scripture and experiences from his own life as a father and husband, Glenn Stanton seeks to equip parents to encourage their children in the gender God has given them. Whether your kids are younger or older, this book shows parents how to relate to their sons and daughters in appropriate ways and help them fulfill their specific callings and destinies. Included in his book are topics such as talking to your children about sex, sexuality and gender roles. Through his relaxed style, Glenn Stanton gives his readers the information they need to empower their children to be the man or woman God intended them to be. With all the gender issues we see in the media and our culture, this book is an excellent guidebook for parents to counteract the underhanded agenda of gender-confusion targeted at our children.

POINTER: Glenn mentions a handful of other books throughout his text. Please note that some of these books are not written by Christian authors, but he has referenced them because they contain pearls of wisdom.

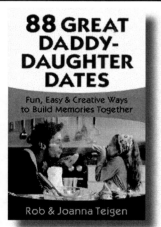

88 Great Daddy-Daughter Dates

by Rob & Joanna Tiegen

Full of great ideas for dates with your daughter, this book will make it easy to spend meaningful father-daughter time. Rob and Joanna Teigen have packed this book full of ideas taken from their own family, as well as including principles from scripture to share with your daughter. Included with each date idea are conversation starters you can use to spark meaningful conversation with your precious girl.

POINTER: This book makes spending daddy-daughter time something that's easy to implement and fun. While you don't have to read the book cover to cover, we highly suggest reading the introduction, as the author has spelled out some excellent tips for a dad trying to connect with his daughter.

Notes

Notes

4th Grade Intro

As your child grows closer to the teen years, use every opportunity to connect with him or her in a positive way. Kids at this age want mom and dad to spend time with them, to tell them what is right and wrong, and to involve themselves in their lives. Mom and dad, you are really important to your children! They may not always show it, but your children need your guidance and support now more than ever. They are changing and growing every day, and some of these changes can be scary to them. Their brains are developing at a rapid rate, which means they are thinking of new things they have never thought of before now. Don't miss out on opportunities to discuss and share with them. They need an outlet for all their new thoughts and ideas, and who better to talk with them than mom and dad?

Memory Verse
"I beseech you therefore, brethren, by the mercies of God, that you present your bodies a living sacrifice, holy, acceptable to God, which is your reasonable service. And do not be conformed to this world, but be transformed by the renewing of your mind, that you may prove what is that good and acceptable and perfect will of God." Romans 12:1-2 (NKJV)

Media Discernment

This is an appropriate age to address issues of censorship and setting one's self apart from the crowd. Around this age, your children may start to wonder why they can't see certain things or participate in certain activities that their friends can. Now is a good age to explain why you are protecting them from some of the things their friends get to experience and why you feel they need to be protected from such things. I went to a Christmas party a few years ago at a neighbor's house up the street from ours. I brought my 9- and 6-year-old girls with me. At this party, the kids were playing downstairs, so I had my husband go down and settle my kids in with the other ones. A while later, my oldest daughter came upstairs and told me that she did not think she should be down there because the other children were watching *Legally Blonde 2*, a movie that she had not heard of, but knew she probably should not be watching.

The point of this story is that it is important to reinforce values of censorship and discretion at home at an early age so that when your children are in a potentially compromising situation, they will know what to do. If your children know what is wrong and why it's important to protect oneself from questionable material, they will choose the right thing to do even if it's different from what everyone else is doing. Also, your children will be able to respond correctly even when we as parents are not there to protect them. It is extremely important that you explain to your children that you and your family choose to be set apart from the crowd. However, take caution to not sound judgmental when you talk about other families and their decisions.

Spiritual Development

Along with new thoughts about the world and their own lives, your child is going to have new thoughts and questions about God. You'll notice that the same answers that used to satisfy their curiosity about spiritual matters when they were 5 are no longer going to be sufficient for them now. As new questions and thoughts pop up, show them how to go to the Bible for their answers. Take advantage of their curiosity by showing them that no matter what question they have, God's Word has answers!

Godly Sexuality

This year we feature the *Beautifully Made! Series* for girls and *The Wonderful Way Babies Are Made* for boys and girls. These two resources talk about the glory of God's creation and His design for the human body. Use discretion with your children as you are sharing these sensitive issues with them. If the subject of sexuality makes them uncomfortable, be careful not to mention anything in front of their friends or in front of other parents that is going to embarrass your children. They will trust you to talk to them about issues of sexuality if they know you are a discreet and sensitive source.

Teachable Moments

My second oldest daughter was babysitting two young boys with a friend of hers, a boy about the same age as my daughter. Things were going relatively well until one of the little boys asked my daughter when she and her friend were going to kiss. Taken aback, my daughter was not sure how to respond. I stepped in at that moment and explained to the boys that they were not going to kiss because they are each—individually—waiting for their wedding days to kiss. The situation brought to mind the fact that I need to be sensitive and supportive of my kids when situations arise that are awkward or potentially hurtful to them. There are situations where our kids are going to feel embarrassed or even be ridiculed because of the stance they've taken for purity. But we, as parents, need to reaffirm them when they face these situations. They need to know that they are not wrong—our culture is.

4TH GRADE ORGANIZER

Tools for the Sandbox

- [ ] *A Boy after God's Own Heart*
      by Jim George
- [ ] *His Mighty Warrior*
      by Sheri Rose Shepherd
- [ ] *His Little Princess*
      by Sheri Rose Shepherd
- [ ] *Sword Fighting*
      by Karyn Henley
- [ ] *The Wonderful Way Babies Are Made*
      by Larry Christenson
- [ ] *Beautifully Made! Series*
      edited by Julie Hiramine
- [ ] *King Me*
      by Steve Farrar
- [ ] *Project Blessing* (see page 11)
      by Kay and Julie Hiramine
- [ ] *Six Ways to Keep the Good in Your Boy*
      by Dannah Gresh
- [ ] *Six Ways to Keep the Little in Your Girl*
      by Dannah Gresh

Message in a Bottle

_____

_____

_____

_____

_____

_____

Lifeguard Watch - *Things your children should learn this year*

- [ ] God cares about us in a personal way
- [ ] We can go to God with every feeling and thought we have
- [ ] It's important to pray everyday
- [ ] It's essential to study your Bible everyday
- [ ] God designed sex for marriage
- [ ] Basic concept of what sex is
- [ ] Basic concept of how babies develop
- [ ] How your body is going to change

- [ ] God created all living things to reproduce in a similar way
- [ ] Mom and Dad are the source of information about sex and sexuality
- [ ] If I have a question about sex or body changes, I should ask Mom or Dad
- [ ] I should strive to be a good steward of the things God has given me
- [ ] God wants me to respect authority

Just Joining Us?

If this is your first year doing the *Against the Tide* curriculum, there are a few resources we recommend starting with, before you jump into this year's resources:

- *Before I Was Born* (description on page 53)
- *Knights, Maidens and Dragons* (description on page 55)
- *The Princess and the Kiss* (description on page 19)
- *The Squire and the Scroll* (description on page 21)
- *Guardians of Purity* (description on page 10)

TIMELINE OPTIONS

Option 1 – Week Study

Start each day by having your child repeat the memory verse back to you. Your goal is to have them saying the verse from memory by the end of the week.

Day 1: First half of *The Wonderful Way Babies Are Made* and one letter from *His Little Princess* and/or *His Mighty Warrior**

Day 2: Second half of *The Wonderful Way Babies Are Made* and one letter from *His Little Princess* and/or *His Mighty Warrior*

Day 3: One devotion from *Sword Fighting**, one letter from *His Little Princess* and/or *His Mighty Warrior*, and the first chapter of *A Boy after God's Own Heart*.

Day 4: One devotion from *Sword Fighting*, one letter from *His Little Princess* and/or *His Mighty Warrior*, and the second chapter of *A Boy after God's Own Heart*.

Day 5: *Beautifully Made!* and/or the third chapter of *A Boy after God's Own Heart*, one devotion from *Sword Fighting*, and one letter from *His Little Princess* and/or *His Mighty Warrior*

*You will not be able to complete *His Little Princess* and/or *His Mighty Warrior*, *Sword Fighting*, or *A Boy after God's Own Heart* in one week. We will have taken you through 5 letters in *His Little Princess* and/or *His Mighty Warrior*, which leaves you with about 45 to finish. These letters are short and sweet, though, and will doubtless make a great addition to your family devotion times or bedtime reading. *Sword Fighting* features an entire year of devotions. We will be taking you through 3 days of devotions, leaving you the rest to integrate into the remainder of your school year. Finally, *A Boy after God's Own Heart* contains 10 chapters, so after the week long study is over, you will have 7 left.

Option 2 – Unit Study

Start each session by having your child recite the memory verse with you. Your goal is to have them saying the verse from memory by the end of the unit.

Week 1: *The Wonderful Way Babies Are Made*, 12 letters from *His Little Princess* and/or *His Mighty Warrior*, and 2 chapters of *A Boy after God's Own Heart*.

Week 2: 7 devotions from *Sword Fighting**, 13 letters from *His Little Princess* and/or *His Mighty Warrior*, and 3 chapters of *A Boy after God's Own Heart*.

Week 3: 7 devotions from *Sword Fighting*, 13 letters from *His Little Princess* and/or *His Mighty Warrior*, and 2 chapters of *A Boy after God's Own Heart*.

Week 4: *Beautifully Made!*, 7 devotions from *Sword Fighting*, 12 letters from *His Little Princess* and/or *His Mighty Warrior*, and 3 chapters of *A Boy after God's Own Heart*.

Sword Fighting features an entire year of devotions for children. We will be taking you through 3 weeks of these devotions in this unit study, so you will have 49 weeks left to complete afterward. These devotions are quick and simple, so they will be easy to implement into the rest of your school year.

Option 3 – Family Devos

Be sure to recite your memory verse at the beginning or end of your family devotion time.

The following children's books are appropriate to incorporate into your regular family devotion time:
His Mighty Warrior and/or *His Little Princess*
Sword Fighting
A Boy after God's Own Heart

THE WONDERFUL WAY BABIES ARE MADE

by Larry Christenson

This is a wonderful book for kids 3-10. The big text is for younger kids, while the text in the boxes should be saved for older, more mature kids. Each set of text communicates the wonder of God's creation as it tells the story of how God created the world, how He made plants, animals, people, and families, and the wonderful way He makes babies. We love this book because it gives children a Godly, positive perspective on creation and life in general. It also has a profound section on adoption and explains how Jesus was adopted by Joseph and Mary. We have utilized this book in previous grades because it does an excellent job helping children establish a healthy view of the glory of God's creation.

Read the small print (in the boxes) with your child. Afterward, ask your child if he or she has any questions for you. Remember to emphasize that if he or she has any questions about sex or sexuality, you are the one to ask. By reading this book with your child, you will communicate that you are a trustworthy and willing source for information, and will thereby prevent your child from seeking another source.

DISCUSSION QUESTIONS

Why do you think God designed living things to reproduce like this?

Read the story of creation found in Genesis chapter 1. Ask your child: Are there any parts of this passage that you understand better after reading **The Wonderful Way Babies Are Made?**

God puts us into our families for a reason. Are you thankful He put you in the family He did?

If you have ultrasound pictures from when your child was in the womb, share them with him or her.

Letters from God

HIS MIGHTY WARRIOR (for boys)

by Sheri Rose Shepherd

This collection of love letters written from God to your son is sure to guide his heart to please and honor the Lord. Full of Scripture and heartfelt encouragement, your son will learn what it means to be a mighty warrior in God's army. In its illustrated pages, your son will learn about servanthood, coming to God in prayer, confessing his sins, who he is in Christ, respecting authority, and many more Biblical lessons. On the pages opposite the letters from the King, your son will find a response that he can use as a prayer.

POINTER: This quick read can be used as a daily devotional or inspiring bed-time reading. Because the letters are relatively short, your son can even read them on his own for some one-on-one devotional time with God.

DISCUSSION QUESTIONS

Do you think God can talk to people in this way, as if He were writing them a letter?	*How can you have a constant conversation with God?*
What other things has God written to you?	*Do you ask Him for help with the things you do everyday?*

HIS LITTLE PRINCESS (for girls)

by Sheri Rose Shepherd

This charming book is a compilation of love letters written from God to your daughter. In these touching letters, your daughter will learn what it means to be a true daughter of the King. Each of the fifty letters from the King contains a good lesson your daughter can ruminate on throughout her day as she strives to make her character reflect her identity as a child of God. The lessons include having a good attitude despite difficult circumstances, having a good body image, the importance of selflessness, the gift of prayer and worship, the beauty of God's creation, dealing with fear, watching one's words, resisting temptation, repentance, and so on. Each letter from the King also contains a Bible verse your daughter can use to memorize and meditate on the lesson she's learned that day. Opposite the letter from the King is a letter in response your daughter can read as a prayer.

POINTER:

This is an excellent resource to use as a devotional to teach your daughter the habit of daily prayer, or as a bed-time story she can read with you as you help her with her prayer times. Because of the relatively short length of the letters, your daughter can also use this book for one-on-one devotional time.

DISCUSSION QUESTIONS

Do you think God can talk to people in this way, as if He were writing them a letter?	*How can you have a constant conversation with God?*
What other things has God written to you?	*Do you ask Him for help with the things you do everyday?*

A Boy after God's Own Heart (for boys)

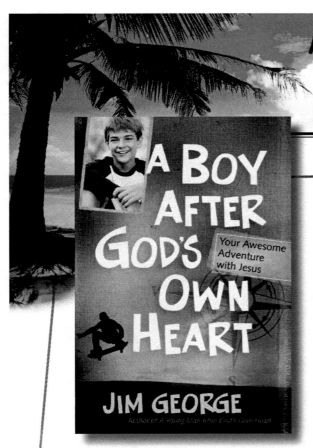

by Jim George

Jim George invites boys to visit 10 areas of their lives: heart, space, parents, family, school, friends, church, self, time, and relationship with Jesus in this quick read. Boys will get God's perspective on all these topics, including advice from a man who has lived out the principles he writes about.

Taking wisdom from scripture and telling the story of Dylan, a boy doing his best to follow God, Jim encourages boys to give their whole lives to the Lord. Each chapter includes prayers, journal topics, and verses to reflect on.

Ask your son what is something new he's learned from this book. If he's comfortable, ask him to share what he learned at the dinner table. Several of the topics in this book are probably things or lessons he's heard before, but perhaps he's read a new insight or understands something better because of the book. If your son has a hard time coming up with something, ask him the discussion questions below to jog his memory.

POINTER

DISCUSSION QUESTIONS

Think about your friends. What do you appreciate about each one of your friends?

What was your favorite chapter from this book? Why?

Were you able to relate to Dylan from this book? What ways are you similar to Dylan? Was there anything he dealt with that you also have to deal with?

Beautifully Made! Series (for girls)

Edited by Julie Hiramine

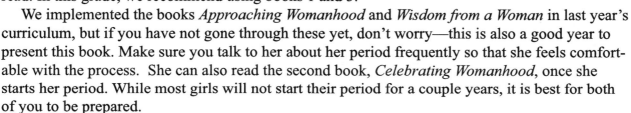

Beautifully Made! is a three-book series designed to guide girls and their mothers through the transition from girlhood to womanhood. These books specifically talk about body changes and starting your first period. The first book, *Approaching Womanhood*, is for moms and their daughters to read together, before the start of the daughter's first period. Book 2, *Celebrating Womanhood*, is for the daughter when she starts her first period, and Book 3, *Wisdom from a Woman*, is just for mom to read. In this grade, we recommend using books 1 and 3.

We implemented the books *Approaching Womanhood* and *Wisdom from a Woman* in last year's curriculum, but if you have not gone through these yet, don't worry—this is also a good year to present this book. Make sure you talk to her about her period frequently so that she feels comfortable with the process. She can also read the second book, *Celebrating Womanhood*, once she starts her period. While most girls will not start their period for a couple years, it is best for both of you to be prepared.

If you have not read the third book, *Wisdom from a Woman*, be sure to read this one before you go through *Approaching Womanhood* with your daughter. It is full of practical advice and encouragement for mom as she prepares a discussion on growing up and maturing with her daughter.

Be sensitive about the subject of menstruation with your daughter. Don't discuss it in front of her friends or with other moms if it makes your daughter uncomfortable. Most girls need some time to get comfortable with their body changes, and your discretion will be a great relief to your daughter.

Discussion Questions

> *Can you describe in your own words what a menstrual cycle is?*

> *Why is modesty important? Ask your mom to discuss the topic of modesty with you.*

> *Why do you think God created women's bodies to function this way?*

Another fun activity is to go bra shopping with your daughter. Make it a special date where just you and she can go have a fun day together. Because some girls develop earlier than others, we put this activity in early. Just go whenever she starts to develop.

SWORD FIGHTING

by Karyn Henley

This is a treasure of Bible study for children ages 6-10. Karyn has organized a year-long Bible study plan that kids can study with their siblings, their parents, even their friends. Organized by week, each chapter features a memory verse and then 7 days of Bible study. For each day, Karyn has thought-provoking discussion questions and engaging activities and object lessons to help children understand the richness of God's Word. Your children will enjoy spending quality time studying God's Word, while also interacting with others as they learn to understand deep truths.

Sword Fighting references the *Day By Day Kid's Bible* for Bible reading. You can find this Bible on www.karynhenley.com. Although she references this Bible throughout the book, she also gives you specific scripture references, so you can use your Bible of choice.

Six Ways to Keep the Good in Your Boy
by Dannah Gresh

The age range of 8-12 for boys is incredibly important - it's a time where mom and dad need to ramp up their training, tune into what the culture is trying to throw at them, and generally help their boy stay "good". While this isn't an easy task, it is one that comes with great rewards. Dannah shows readers how to lovingly engage their sons over many points that come up during adolescence: body changes and the birds and the bees, unplugging and experiencing the real world God created, and giving him vision for the future and a sense of purpose. Dannah shows you how you can connect with your son and keep your relationship open during his teen years and beyond.

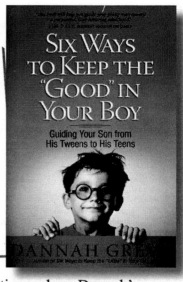

POINTER: While this book was written to moms, there are several sections where Dannah's husband, Bob, chimes in and gives pointers to dads, too. Also included are tips from Angela Thomas, a single mom who shares from her own experience to give help and encouragement to other single moms.

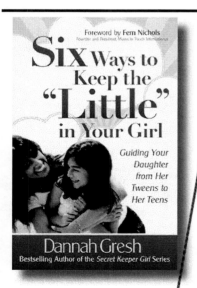

Six Ways to Keep the Little in Your Girl
by Dannah Gresh

There is so much pressure on our girls to grow up too fast. Whether it's the clothes being sold, the lyrics of the most popular songs among youth, or the characters protrayed in popular movies, girls are bombarded with unsavory messages about who they are and what they should be doing. Dannah gives moms hope and encouragement as she addresses issues like modesty, giving your daughter "the talk", sheltering her from harmful media, and protecting her body image. This book is all about allowing your daughter to flourish and grow at the pace God designed for her - and Dannah shows how moms can encourage healthy growth in their daughters.

POINTER: Also included in Dannah's book is her husband Bob's perspective on raising daughters in today's culture. These points are really good for dad to read! Dannah also provides some really good ideas for activities you can do with your daughter.

King Me

by Steve Farrar

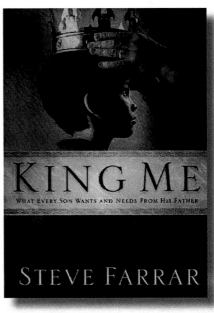

Steve does an excellent job in this book of teaching fathers how to mentor their sons. He addresses a wide range of issues from discipline to sexual purity. By examining the kings of the Bible, he pulls examples not only from the things they did correctly, but also from the things that were displeasing to the Lord. Included in this book is instruction for how to be the authority in your home, while still being gracious, loving, and humble. One of the many pearls of wisdom in this book is his approach to giving privileges as a response to responsible behavior. This is an excellent book for the dad who wants to be intentional about mentoring and guiding his son during the preteen and teen years.

Pointer:

Steve Farrar is an excellent writer who includes real-life stories into his teaching. The strong point of Steve's book is his thorough approach to blessing your children by your example in Godly manhood and intentional discipleship.

Notes

RESOURCE GUIDE

BOOKS NOT TO MISS FOR GIRLS:

- *A Little Book of Manners for Girls: Courtesy & Kindness for Young Ladies* by Emilie Barnes, Harvest House Publishers
- *A Little Girl after God's Own Heart* by Elizabeth George, Harvest House Publishers
- *Beautifully Made! Approaching Womanhood (Book One)* edited by Julie Hiramine, Generations of Virtue
- *Beautifully Made! Celebrating Womanhood (Book Two)* edited by Julie Hiramine, Generations of Virtue
- *Good Manners for a Little Princess* by Kelly Chapman, Harvest House Publishers
- *His Little Princess* by Sheri Rose Shepherd, WaterBrook Multnomah Publishing Group
- *I'd Be Your Princess* by Kathryn O'Brien, Standard Publishing
- *Just Mom and Me Having Tea* by Mary J. Murray, Harvest House Publishers
- *Lady in Waiting for Little Girls* by Jackie Kendall and Dede Kendall, New Hope Publishers
- *Princess Grace and the Little Lost Kitten, Princess Joy's Birthday Blessing, Princess Faith's Mysterious Garden, Princess Hope and the Hidden Treasure,* and *Princess Charity's Courageous Heart* by Jeanna Young and Jacqueline Johnson, Zondervan Publishing House
- *Princess with a Purpose* by Kelly Chapman, Harvest House Publishers
- *The Princess and the Three Knights* by Karen Kingsbury, Zondervan Publishing House

BOOKS NOT TO MISS FOR BOYS:

- *A Boy after God's Own Heart* by Jim George, Harvest House Publishers
- *A Little Book of Manners for Boys* by Bob and Emilie Barnes, Harvest House Publishers
- *A Little Boy after God's Own Heart* by Jim and Elizabeth George, Harvest House Publishers
- *A Warrior Prince for God* by Kelly Chapman, Harvest House Publishers
- *God's Mighty Warrior Devotional Bible* by Sheila Walsh, Thomas Nelson Publishers
- *His Mighty Warrior* by Sheri Rose Shepherd, WaterBrook Multnomah Publishing
- *Good Manners for a Little Warrior* by Kelly Chapman, Harvest House Publishers
- *I'd Be Your Hero* by Kathryn O'Brien, Standard Publishing
- *Will, God's Mighty Warrior* by Sheila Walsh, Thomas Nelson Publishers
- *The Brave Young Knight* by Karen Kingsbury, Zondervan Publishing House

You can order all these resources online at:
www.generationsofvirtue.org

RESOURCE GUIDE

BOOKS NOT TO MISS FOR BOYS AND GIRLS:

- *Before I Was Born* by Carolyn Nystrom, NavPress
- *Character Building from the Life of Jesus* by V. Gilbert Beers, Campus Crusade Asia
- *Everyday Graces* edited by Karen Santorum, Intercollegiate Studies Institute
- *Knights, Maidens and Dragons* by Julia Duin, Chalfont House
- *My Big Book of 5-Minute Devotions* by Pamela Kennedy with Douglas Kennedy, Ideals Publications
- *Sword Fighting* by Karyn Henley, Child Sensitive Communications
- *The Princess and the Kiss* by Jennie Bishop, Warner Press
- *The Squire and the Scroll* by Jennie Bishop, Warner Press
- *The Story of Me* by Stan and Brenna Jones, NavPress
- *The Swimsuit Lesson* by Jon Holsten, Holsten Books
- *The Wonderful Way Babies Are Made* by Larry Christenson, Bethany House Publishers
- *Why Do Birds Build Nests?* by Susan Horner, Moody Publishers
- *Why Do Plants Grow?* by Susan Horner, Moody Publishers

BOOKS NOT TO MISS FOR PARENTS:

- *88 Great Daddy-Daughter Dates* by Rob and Joanna Tiegen, Revell Publishers
- *Beautifully Made! Wisdom from a Woman: Mother's Guide (Book Three)* edited by Julie Hiramine, Generations of Virtue
- *Guardians of Purity* by Julie Hiramine, Charisma House Publishers
- *Just Mom and Me Having Tea* by Mary J. Murray, Harvest House Publishers
- *King Me* by Steve Farrar, Moody Publishers
- *Loving Our Kids on Purpose* by Danny Silk, Destiny Image Publishers
- *Preparing Him for the Other Woman* by Sheri Rose Shepherd, WaterBrook Multnomah Publishing Group
- *Project Blessing* by Kay and Julie Hiramine, Generations of Virtue
- *Raising a Daughter after God's Own Heart* by Elizabeth George, Harvest House Publishers
- *Secure Daughters, Confident Sons* by Glenn T. Stanton, WaterBrook Multonomah Publishers
- *Shepherding a Child's Heart* by Tedd Tripp, Shepherd Press
- *Six Ways to Keep the Good in Your Boy* by Dannah Gresh and Bob Gresh, Harvest House Publishers
- *Six Ways to Keep the Little in Your Girl* by Dannah Gresh, Harvest House Publishers
- *The Father Connection* by Josh McDowell, B&H Publishing Group

> *You can order all these resources online at: www.generationsofvirtue.org*

About
GENERATIONS OF VIRTUE

Generations of Virtue is a non-profit, wholly volunteer ministry dedicated to equipping parents and young people to boldly stand for purity in our world today.

WE SPECIALIZE IN:

- CHARACTER DEVELOPMENT

- PURITY BOOKS AND RESOURCES FOR ALL AGES

- AN EXTENSIVE LINE OF EXCLUSIVE PURITY JEWELRY

- INTERNATIONAL MINISTRY

- INTERNSHIP PROGRAMS

AND SO MUCH MORE!

VISIT US ONLINE FOR THE BEST SELECTION OF PURITY RESOURCES ON THE WEB!
WWW.GENERATIONSOFVIRTUE.ORG

YOUR PURCHASES AID IN BRINGING THE MESSAGE OF PURITY TO THOUSANDS OF FAMILIES WORLDWIDE. THANK YOU FOR SUPPORTING OUR MINISTRY!

Continue the training with your preteens and teenagers with

AGAINST THE TIDE

middle school

If you enjoyed *Against the Tide* for elementary students, check out *Against the Tide* for middle-schoolers! Organized by gender, this guide will take you through curriculum for 10-14 year-old boys and girls. It's the same approach to purity training from your trusted ministry for purity resources—only for older children!

Catching them at their most impressionable stages, your children will learn about:

God's design for romance and marriage

Staying pure in our immoral Cultu

Discerning the messages in media

Being a positive influence amongst their peer

Standing Against the Tide!

Finally! A website designed with you in mind.

www.generationsofvirtue.org

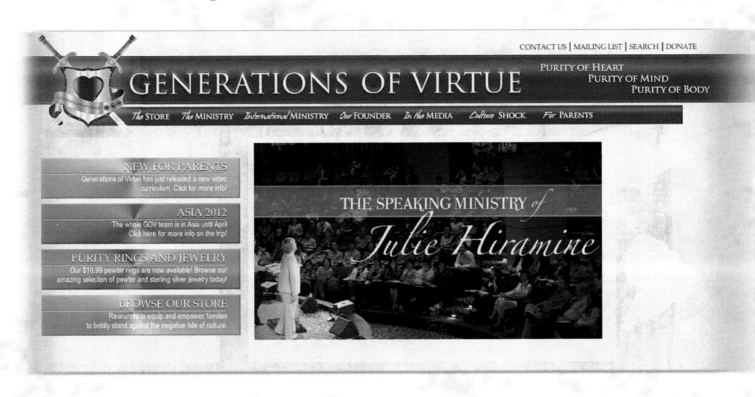

Fun and Informative!

Tips for parents!

Your purity destination HQ!

Great for teens!

www.generationsofvirtue.org

Extensive product selection from the purity experts!